CHILDREN CELEBRATE!

CHILDREN CELEBRATE!

Activity-based ideas for round-the-year worship

• • •

Joan Chapman

Illustrations by Yvonne Bell

Marshall Pickering
An Imprint of HarperCollins*Publishers*

Marshall Pickering is an Imprint of
HarperCollins*Religious*
Part of HarperCollins*Publishers*
77–85 Fulham Palace Road, London W6 8JB

First published in Great Britain
in 1994 by Marshall Pickering

10 9 8 7 6 5 4 3 2 1

A catalogue record for this book is
available from the British Library

ISBN 0 551 02866-1

Typeset by Harper Phototypesetters Limited
Northampton, England
Printed and bound in Great Britain by
Scotprint Limited, Edinburgh

Illustrations by Yvonne Bell

I wish to dedicate *Children Celebrate!* to
my beloved Father and Mother whose love
and support have provided inspiration for
this and much, much more.

CONTENTS

INTRODUCTION   xi

1   **CELEBRATING**   1
Why, what and how do we celebrate?
The wedding at Cana
John 2:1-12

2   **GOD LOVES US: HE MADE US AND ALL CREATION**   4
Celebrating the wonder of God's gift of creation and remembering
our responsibility for its care
The Creation story
Genesis 1

3   **GOD LOVES US: HE FEEDS US — HARVEST FESTIVAL**   8
We celebrate and give thanks for the wonder of Harvest
Moses and manna from Heaven
Exodus 16

4   **GOD LOVES US SO WE TRY TO FOLLOW HIM**   10
What is a Christian? How do we try to do God's will?
The road to Damascus
Acts 9:1-20

5   **BAPTISM**   14
We make a commitment to love and serve God
John baptizes Jesus
Matthew 3:13-17

6   **ALL SAINTS**   18
What makes a saint? Can we be like them?
A modern-day saint — Mother Teresa

7   **PATRON SAINTS**   22
St Andrew, St David, St Patrick and St George

8   **REMEMBRANCE SUNDAY**   27
Remembering the dreadfulness of war so that we may strive to
prevent further suffering
Love one another
Luke 6:27-38

9 THE BIBLE 30
The greatest source of knowledge in our relationship with God

10 HANUKAH 34
A Jewish festival, celebrated by Jesus, when they remember the defeat
of their enemies, the return of their sacred Temple to God's worship
and the re-dedication of their own lives to God
Judas Maccabeus

11 ADVENT 39
Getting ready time — preparation for Christmas
The Annunciation
Luke 1:26-38

12 CHRISTINGLE 45
A comparatively new festival to Britain

13 CHRISTMAS 47
One of the great festivals of the year — remembering the birth of Jesus
The Christmas story
Luke 2:4-20

14 NEW YEAR AND EPIPHANY 50
A fresh start — visitors who influence our lives
The visit of the Wise Men
Matthew 2:1-15

15 CANDLEMAS 53
Jesus, the Light of the world
The presentation of Jesus in the Temple
Luke 2:21-40

16 JESUS THE TEACHER AND HEALER 56
Celebrating the life and work of Jesus
The Lord's Prayer
Matthew 6:9-13

17 THE GOOD SAMARITAN 58
One of Jesus' best known stories
The Good Samaritan
Luke 10:25-37

18 JESUS, FRIEND OF SINNERS 60
God loves us and forgives us even when we do wrong
The Prodigal Son
Luke 15:11—32

19 SHROVE TUESDAY, ASH WEDNESDAY AND LENT 63
Preparation for the greatest festival in the Church year
The temptation of Jesus in the wilderness
Matthew 4:1-11; Luke 4:1-13

20 **FRIENDS** 68
Exploring what it is to be a true friend
The four friends
Luke 5:17–26

21 **PASSOVER** 71
The feast that celebrates the Israelites' escape from Egyptian oppression
Escape from Egypt
Exodus 8 to 12

22 **MOTHERING SUNDAY** 74
Ruth and Naomi
Book of Ruth

23 **HOLY WEEK AND EASTER** 77
Explore and celebrate the events that lead up to the greatest festival
of the Christian year, and celebrate Easter itself
Palm Sunday
Entry into Jerusalem and the cleansing of the Temple
Matthew 21:1–17

Maundy Thursday
The Last Supper and the Garden of Gethsemane
Mark 14:12–51

Good Friday
Trial and Crucifixion
Matthew 27; Mark 15; Luke 23; John 18:12–19:42

Easter Day
Easter morning
Matthew 28; Mark 16; Luke 24; John 20

24 **CHRISTIAN MISSION AND AID AGENCIES** 87
Christian agencies who give aid throughout the world
The parable of the sheep and the goats
Matthew 25:31–46

25 **ASCENSION** 92
The feast of the Ascension and God's promise to be with us always
The Ascension
Acts 1:1–11

26 **SHAVUOT** 95
Explore the Jewish festival of Shavuot and its implications for Christians
The Ten Commandments given to Moses
Exodus 19 and 20

27 **PENTECOST** 99
Explore and celebrate the 'birthday' of the Church
The Spirit comes to the Apostles
Acts 2:1–11

28 **TRINITY**   104
Explore what Trinity means and celebrate the 'Three in One'

29 **ST PETER**   107
Explore the life of St Peter and his influence on the Christian Church
Peter denies knowing Jesus
Matthew 26:31-35 and 69-75

30 **MUSIC**   111
Celebrate the joy of music
Psalm 150

31 **GARDENS AND FLOWERS**   114
Celebrate the joy brought by flowers and gardens, their use in food,
medicine and cosmetics, as well as the 'language of flowers'
Consider the lilies of the field
Luke 12:27-31

32 **WINNING AND LOSING**   119
Explore what it is to win and lose — the effect on others around us
in our responses to success and failure
The parable of the talents
Matthew 25:14—30

33 **ANIMALS**   122
Celebrating the companionship and interest shared with animals
Noah and the ark
Genesis 7 and 8

34 **HOLIDAYS**   126
The need for rest and relaxation and celebrating all the opportunities
that holidays give
Feeding the 5,000
Matthew 14:13-21; Mark 6:30-44

35 **LOOKING BACK AND MOVING ON**   128
At the end of term, remembering what is good; preparing to take that
on whilst acknowledging the fears and apprehension of facing change
Philip and the Ethiopian
Acts 8:4-6, 26-40

PUZZLE ANSWERS   131

INTRODUCTION

Children Celebrate! was written in response to the search of children's work leaders for more material to use with children which was simple and easy to use. Children's work in churches has so many restrictions — lack of space, poor funding or support, time, wide age range, spasmodic attendance etc. *Children Celebrate!* seeks to offer help to the busy children's work leader and to the children with whom we try to share our faith. The image of the dedicated teacher with children at her feet is still there but the emphasis is now on *shared* faith, rather than the teacher and the taught, exploring together our faith and the Story on which it is based.

Children Celebrate! is the voice of one who wants to share something very special:

- belief that God is love
- the Story that confirms that belief
- a desire to express that belief in worship.

The words are directed towards the child — not just the child in years. Belief is not based on intellect and reason which can be argued away but on experience and trust formed from that experience. Our reponses are based on our own chemical and emotional make-up. We are all touched by different experiences. We need to offer stimulus that may reach out to all our senses, not just satisfy our intellect. In recent times the Church has sometimes forgotten some of the rich sensual stimuli that were used in the Middle Ages. We need to restore what was good in that. The present-day Church covers such a wide variety of styles, but one faith. Let us use the best — whatever suits our temperament — to reach out, explore and worship.

Children need to feel loved and treasured — respected for what they are, not what we would like them to be. They often show great insight that may surprise the unwary adult and, as the report *Children in the Way* suggests, they may just hold the 'fragment of map' missing from our own in our faith search.

The language in *Children Celebrate!* is simple enough for even a small child to understand, but hopefully does not 'talk down' to them. I prefer to think that we reach up to their understanding — after all it is difficult to explain things in simple terms sometimes and we really have to explore what it means in order to do that without 'watering down' the true meaning.

As *Children in the Way* showed so graphically, we take in only 10 per cent of what we hear, but 90 per cent of what we *do*. All learning can and should be FUN — but that does not mean that we do not take our faith seriously. Exploration can take many different forms and the activities in *Children Celebrate!* are as varied as possible. Most of these activities could be used effectively with all ages, including adults. Many adults are only too pleased to be given the opportunity to use activities — music, drama, art and craft to explore their faith rather than just cerebral or passive listening.

There are 35 sessions which essentially cover the festivals and seasons of the Church year. Many sessions have enough material for more than one week's work; Holy Week and the Easter story in particular have enough material to cover several sessions or a holiday club. Some sessions are not related to any particular time in the year and can be slotted into your programme wherever it is convenient.

Each session comprises:
• Introduction and background information
• Story — usually a Bible story
• Activities — a choice, in which there should be something for everybody
• Prayer and Praise

Bible stories are from the *Children's Bible Story Book* told by Jennifer Rees Larcombe, published by HarperCollins (page references are given). The activities require minimum preparation and the variety of suggestions allows for any particular age group. They can also be done by children themselves.

'Prayer and Praise' varies to allow for different styles of worship. Sometimes a simple litany is included, at other times there are more active prayer ideas — reinforcing the theory that prayer is not just 'hands together and eyes closed'. Unless otherwise stated, hymns/songs are taken from *Junior Praise* (numbers 1-301) and *Junior Praise 2* (numbers 302-503), published by Marshall Pickering. Some sessions draw hymns/songs from *Carol Praise* and/or *Mission Praise* (both Marshall Pickering).

You may wish to collect the following to make up a basic store:
• paper and card in assorted colours and sizes
• powder paints in black, white and primary colours
• scissors
• glue (PVA)
• pencils
• rolls of wallpaper to use for backing
• split-pin fasteners
• candles
• felt pens
• scrap material
• ruler

Other occasional stores:
• tissue and crêpe paper in assorted colours
• sticky-back plastic (transparent film)
• wire coat hangers
• wool/string
• needle and thread
• compass

Card and paper can sometimes be obtained from local firms who otherwise throw them out.

One

CELEBRATING

INTRODUCTION

If you look up the word 'celebrating' in your dictionary you will find something like: 'doing something to show that a day or an event is special'. We celebrate our birthdays. Every year on the anniversary of the day that we were born we remember and celebrate. In every family there are special days to remember. Most celebrations are happy — a time for remembering happy events; perhaps a birthday or wedding anniversary, a new baby or moving into a new house.

Most of us like to celebrate with others — friends and family. We share our fun. Think of the celebrations in your family or community. What have you celebrated in the last year?

Some of those celebrations will have been just in the family but others will have been celebrated all over the country, and even all over the world. Which of these celebrations will be remembered by other families and communities? The Church community celebrates many times in the year and many of these occasions will be celebrated by people all over the world.

Jesus celebrated too. We know that he went up to Jerusalem to celebrate a special feast. We know that he also went to the wedding of friends in Cana. We do not know the names of the friends but we know that Jesus helped to make this a very special celebration.

STORY

> The wedding at Cana
> John 2:1-12
> The wedding that nearly went wrong
> (p. 144)

ACTIVITIES

Photo album of your life
You will need:
- *sheets of coloured sugar paper (or similar)*
- *white paper*
- *scissors, glue, crayons/felt pens*

You do not take photographs of every day in your life. It is only the special days, people and events that you record in an album. The celebration times are when you are likely to take photographs.

Draw pictures for your album. Choose what means most to you. Pictures may include your family and friends, your home/homes, pets, holidays, baptisms and weddings, birthdays, visits, picnics, outings, first day at school etc. etc. You could look at a real photograph album or these suggestions may jog your memory:

- the most important people in my life (family or friends)
- the most important place to me (home or bedroom or a 'den')
- a time when I felt really happy (a visit, picnic etc)
- a time when I felt sad (the death of a pet, or a friend moving away)
- a time when I felt everything went well
- a time when nothing seemed to go right

Fold sheets of coloured paper into an album. Stick your pictures into your album. You may like to make the corners look like photo corners. The drawing could take a long time so you may want to add to this over the weeks.

Remembering journey

Draw your own remembering journey. Draw people who have been very special to you. Places are important: in some places you feel really happy and comfortable; some places give very different memories. You will remember things that you did or things that happened to you that made a difference to you. Draw them along a road that travels through your life. Don't worry if you cannot get them in the right order! Just try to include as many special memories as you can.

Newspaper pictures

You will need lots of newspapers. It is wise to start collecting newspaper pictures well in advance — there are never just the right photographs when you want them! Pictures will need to include national, international and local events/people that have been and maybe still are significant in the lives of many. They may include a wedding, royalty opening something, footballers scoring a goal, etc. Let everybody make their own choice of picture from those collected.

Look carefully at your picture. What is being celebrated in the picture? Have you ever attended the kind of celebration that is recorded in a newspaper? What made it so special? In what ways did you celebrate?

Pretend that you are at the celebration in the picture. Tell your partner/friend what happened. You will have to use · your imagination to feel how the people in the picture feel.

Community Celebration Balloons

You will need:
- *coloured balloons (no patterns. Round balloons are usually easier to blow up than long, thin ones.)*
- *ballpoint pens*
- *string*

When we celebrate it is fun to use balloons. We often have balloons at a party. Think of some of the events that have been celebrated in your community in the past year. Here are some suggestions:

Christmas, Easter, birthdays, Bonfire night, the day the new hall was finished, a wedding, the annual picnic, the Summer Fayre, Harvest Festival, etc.

Together, decide which were important celebrations in the community.

Before you blow up the balloons draw one of the celebrations on each balloon. You could write the name of the celebration on the balloon too. When you blow up the balloon, the picture will be big. Hang up your celebration balloons to remind other people of happy times.

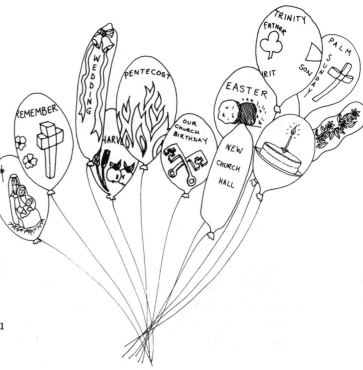

PRAYER AND PRAISE

Father in Heaven, we thank you for all the times we can celebrate and remember. Help us to remember truthfully and celebrate joyfully all the good things you have done for us. Amen.

Thank you, Lord, for all the memories you give me — for people who mean so much to me: friends, relatives and people I meet along the way; for happy times and sad times, exciting times and times when there was not much to interest me. Help me to use my precious memories to be a better follower of you. Amen.

  26 **Clap your hands all you people**
  67 **Hallelu, hallelu**
145 **Jubilate**
202 **Praise him, praise him**
232 **Thank you, Lord**
325 **Come on and celebrate!**
337 **Father God, I wonder**
437 **Oh no! The wine's all gone!**

Two

GOD LOVES US: HE MADE US AND ALL CREATION

INTRODUCTION

Make a small collection of items from God's creation — things that are easily seen and collected on a walk: e.g. leaves, conkers, acorns, beech masts, hazel nuts, stones, shells, seeds, grasses, etc. Include a bunch of flowers (from the garden or flower shop).

If possible, go outside and look around you. Look at the trees and flowers, the insects and birds. Look up at the sky. It may be a beautiful blue or it may be covered with great white clouds. Even in the middle of a big city you can see wonderful things. People are very clever, but if you look around you will see things that even the cleverest human person could not make. Name some of the things you can see.

Christians believe that God made these wonderful things — the sky, the trees, the flowers, the animals; and God even made us! In fact God made the whole world. You can read in the Bible about how the world was made.

STORY

The Creation story
Genesis 1

Many Christians believe this story completely but others believe that God is *still* creating the world now. It doesn't really matter how long it took to make. The important thing is that *God made the world and all that is in it*. Everything we clever humans make is only from the things that God made for us.

ACTIVITIES

Creation drama
You will need:
- *tape recorder*
- *music tape*★
- *different coloured cloths (these could be scarves, old sheets, curtains or large scrap pieces)*
- *animal masks*

Listen to the music and think how the world was made. Let the music help you to re-tell the story. Use the coloured cloths (wrapped round you or waved about) to show the different things that God made:

- white or gold for the light
- black for the darkness
- green for the plants and trees
- brown for the land
- blue for the water

★ The choice of tape is very open but something like:
'Largo' from The New World Symphony by Dvorak
'Morning' from The Peer Gynt Suite by Grieg are very suitable.

Make up your own movement to match the different parts of the story. If you have made flowers and/or animal masks, use them too. You can tell the story in words over the music or simply let the movement and music tell the story.

Animal Masks

There are lots of different ways of making masks but using a paper plate as a base makes it very easy. Choose a creature that you would like to make. The lion mask is one of the easiest, but you can use your imagination to make other animals by cutting and stapling the plate to make a longer nose, add horns and/or ears and, of course, using different colours.

Lion mask

You will need:
- *paper plate*
- *crêpe paper (brown/yellow)*
- *old tights*
- *needle, thread and elastic*
- *scissors and sticky tape*
- *crayon/paints/felt pens*
- *glue*

The underside of the plate will form the face. Colour the underside in a 'lion colour'. Draw in eyes and a place for the nose. Make a small hole for the nose, no more than 1 cm diameter (this may need an adult). Cut a small piece from the tights (about 7 cm square). Make filling from cut-up bits of tights or cotton wool ball. Twist and tie the piece of tights to make a bundle. Poke the free ends of the bundle through the nose hole and secure with tape on the other side. Cut across a fold of crêpe paper. Cut down half the width lots of times to make a fringe. Open out. Stick uncut edge all around the edge of the plate, gathering slightly and easing into place. You will probably require more than one fold of crêpe. Whiskers can be made

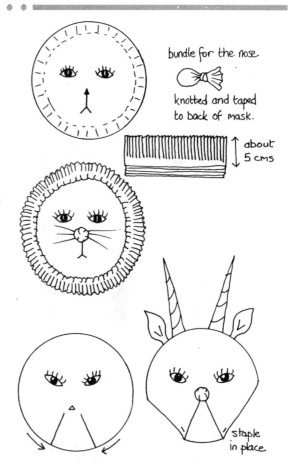

bundle for the nose

knotted and taped to back of mask.

about 5 cms

staple in place

from thread pulled through the nose. Tie some elastic from either side of the mask to hold it against your face.

Tissue flowers

You will need:
- *lots of different coloured tissue paper*
- *art straws (paper drinking straws will do)*
- *green crayon*
- *sticky tape*
- *scissors*

Here is how to make the most basic flower. Flatten a straw and colour it green. (If you are making many flowers use a wax crayon on its side as this is much quicker.) Cut a strip of tissue — about 15 by 5 cm. Fold this into five (or however many is easy). Cut a petal shape from the folded tissue. You will need to hold this firmly as the tissue may slip as you try to cut it. Open out. Gently ease the edge of the tissue which is still held together around the end of

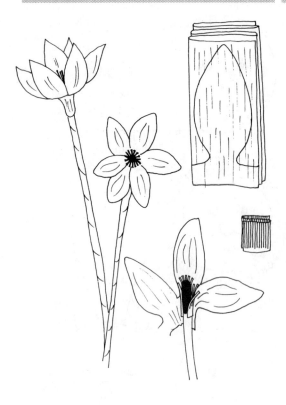

Mix a little powder paint with a little diluted PVA (you will need trial and error to find the right consistency) — blue for the sea, green for the land, brown for the mountains. Use a glue spreader to paint the lantern. When the top half is completely dry turn it over to do the lower half. If you put on several layers, allowing each layer to dry in between, you can build up the mountains so that they stand out. The whole thing will become hard and rigid when it is completely dry and can be kept for use time after time. Hung up over a lamp — the light will shine through.

You can use the same idea on a large piece of hard board. Paint on both sides. If it is hung up and allowed to spin, you will be able to see the whole world on each side of the board.

These globes represent the beautiful world created by God. A piece of netting may be placed over them and covered with signs of human pollution — crisp packets, cigarette ends, etc. — or pictures could be cut out of newspapers showing the ways in which we have spoiled our world. The netting may be rolled back to reveal God's wonderful world underneath.

PRAYER AND PRAISE

Use any of the creation items that were mentioned at the beginning to explore with as many of your senses as possible. For example, hold a flower and look at it very quietly. Look at its colour, shape, beauty. Use your fingers to feel the soft petals, the sharp thorns, the smooth or hairy stems. Smell the scent of the flower.

the straw. (Don't just roll the tissue around it tightly as this means the petals do not spread out well.) Tape the tissue to the straw. Gently draw out the top of each petal. Place your flowers together in a vase. Use your imagination to make lots of different kinds of flowers.

Lamp Shade Globe
You will need:
- *an old, round lamp shade (the lantern type that is made of wire and tissue paper)*
- *PVA ('school') glue*
- *powder paint (blue, brown and green)*
- *an atlas or globe*
- *pencil or pen*

Put the wire frame in place to hold the lantern out rigid. Use an atlas or proper globe to draw the shape of the world on your lantern. (It is quite difficult to reach any degree of accuracy so may need adult help.) Place the lantern in a shallow box so that you have both hands to work with.

Leader	In the beginning, there was darkness. God said:
All	**Let there be light.**
Leader	God separated the light from the darkness. God called the light 'day' and the dark 'night'.
All	**God made the sun and the moon, the stars and the planets.**
Leader	God made the sky, the land and the sea
All	**And it was good.**
Leader	God made plants to grow out of the earth
All	**Plants with leaves and roots, seeds and fruit. God saw that it was good.**
Leader	God said:
All	**Let the waters be filled with all kinds of living creatures and let the air be filled with birds.**
Leader	God made animals of every kind:
Group 1	Large and small,
Group 2	Strong and weak,
Group 3	Animals that climb in the trees,
Group 4	Animals that crawl on the ground,
Group 1	Animals that eat other animals,
Group 2	Animals that eat plants,
Group 3	Animals with soft fur,
Group 4	Animals with coarse hair.
All	**God made all the creatures – reptiles, birds, insects, spiders, amphibians and mammals.**
Leader	Then God made people.
All	**God made me.**
Leader	God made the world and all that is in it.
All	**And it was very good.**

6 **All things bright and beautiful**
48 **For the beauty of the earth**
63 **God who made the earth**
76 **He made the stars to shine**
347 **God in his love for us**
359 **He made the water wet**
415 **Large creatures, small creatures**
419 **Long, long ago**

Three

GOD LOVES US: HE FEEDS US – HARVEST FESTIVAL

INTRODUCTION

God's special people, the Israelites, had been wandering in the desert after they escaped from Egypt. They began to feel hungry so Moses asked God for help.

STORY

Moses and manna from Heaven
Exodus 16

In our country there is no need for anybody to go hungry. God has provided enough for everybody. There are greedy, selfish and ignorant people who sometimes prevent others and even themselves from having the food but God has provided it for us. In many communities, and particularly in Christian churches, we remember how much God loves us and we give thanks for his gifts at Harvest time. At the end of summer or early autumn much of the food that grows naturally is ripe and ready for collecting. In different parts of the country there will be different harvests: some crops grow better in one part of the country than in another. At Harvest time we have our Harvest festival — a celebration of what God has given us.

We don't only remember the farmers' crops either. As well as all the other kinds of foods that we enjoy, we celebrate all God's wonderful gifts — water, coal and gas to make the electricity for so many things in our homes, wool and other products to make fabrics for clothes, wood for paper and furniture . . . There are so many we could make a very long list.

ACTIVITIES

Harvest baskets
You will need:
- *fruit basket or punnet*
- *silver foil or tissue paper*
- *fruit, vegetables and/or flowers*
- *cling film and kitchen towels*
- *cotton wool and rubber bands*

Cover the basket or punnet with silver foil or tissue paper. Arrange the fruit in the basket. It may help to support delicate fruit with kitchen tissues/towels.

Cover the whole of the basket with cling film. If there are any flowers, soak some cotton wool in water and wrap round the end of the stems. Tie in place with a rubber band. Place them on top of the basket.

Harvest collage

Collect food labels off *empty* tins and packets. Look particularly for the country of origin (the place where the contents came from). You will need a large world map. Pin the labels on your map as near to where the product originates. What foods can we grow in our own country? Which foods are we unable to grow here? See how we rely on other countries for much of our food.

Psalm 65

This is a song of praise and thanksgiving to God for his goodness. This psalm is often sung at Harvest time. Try to compose your own psalm/song of praise and thankfulness to God for all the wonderful things he has done for us. You may like to add a verse that asks for forgiveness for our greed in not sharing all this with other parts of the world, where there is not enough. Perhaps you could ask for help in finding ways in which we can learn to share better the resources of the world.

Your psalm/song can be written out carefully, perhaps with an 'illuminated' initial letter for the first word and decorated with pictures of all the things you mention. Gold or silver adds greatly to an illuminated manuscript.

PRAYER AND PRAISE

Use Psalm 65 or your own version of that psalm. Verses 9 to the end are the ones that deal particularly with the theme of Harvest.

Thank you cards

Think of the many great gifts that God gives us at Harvest time. Write or draw them on pieces of card. Each person could bring his or her card to the altar/table and lay it there. You could say aloud some of the things you want to say thank you for or if you are rather shy you can just lay the card on the table.

32 **Come you thankful people**
175 **Now thank we all our God**
193 **Our harvest day is over**
220 **Someone's brought a loaf of bread**
267 **We plough the fields**
311 **At harvest time we celebrate (Celebrate the harvest)**
347 **God in his love for us**

Four

GOD LOVES US SO WE TRY TO FOLLOW HIM

INTRODUCTION

The first Christians were lucky enough to have met and worked with Jesus. Jesus had told them to be like him. They saw how he loved everybody and had even died for them. Some of them had seen Jesus die on a cross. Yet they also saw Jesus alive again. They wanted to go and tell everybody else about Jesus and the great news that God loves us.

At first they had a difficult time. Many of the Jews thought they were wicked and just trying to stir up trouble. The followers of Jesus were persecuted: that means that others tried every possible means to stop them — imprisonment, torture and even execution. Saul was one of the first to persecute Christians but a wonderful experience changed that.

STORY

> The road to Damascus
> Acts 9:1-20
> The man who hated Jesus (p. 192)
> Daring escapes (p. 194)

Saul, or Paul as he became known, was completely changed by his experience. Although he had not met Jesus in the flesh, Paul felt that he knew Jesus and wanted to tell others about his wonderful message. Paul chose to become a follower of Jesus. He became a Christian and was persecuted as he had persecuted others. He had some very difficult experiences and choices to make. Jesus never promised that following him would be easy. Sometimes it is difficult to make the *right* choice. It is often easier or more comfortable to make the wrong decision for Jesus. Are you strong enough to follow what Jesus wants you to do?

ACTIVITIES

What would you do? — Choices game

Print the following 'choices', each on a separate piece of card. They may be used in a 'Snakes and Ladders' form of board game which you can make yourself or simply as a card game on their own.

The discussion of each choice is the important part. Are your choices those that Jesus would make?

You find a £1 coin on the ground. Just as you are going to put it in your pocket, a little girl comes towards you. She is crying and has lost £1.

Do you:

1 Leave the £1 coin in your pocket?

2 Buy her a lolly worth 10p and keep the rest?

3 ?

You and your family are watching TV. You want to watch one programme but your brother/sister/etc wants to watch something else.

Do you:

1 Take charge of the control and refuse to allow others to have it?

2 Allow him/her to watch his/her choice but you sit and sulk or chatter loudly?

3 ?

You have a spelling test. You have not learned the words.

Do you:

1 Look at your neighbour's spelling whilst teacher is not looking?

2 Change the answers after they have been checked?

3 ?

A child is standing alone in the playground looking very unhappy.

Do you:

1 Ignore him/her?

2 Point him/her out to your friends and laugh?

3 ?

Your best friend has forgotten to send you a birthday card?

Do you:

1 Stop being friends with him/her?

2 Tell the rest of your friends that he/she has forgotten?

3 ?

It is wet and cold outside and you have forgotten to feed the rabbit?

Do you:

1 Pretend you haven't remembered?

2 Decide the rabbit can wait until morning?

3 ?

You are halfway through eating a bar of chocolate when your best friend calls.

Do you:

1 Hide it?

2 Stuff it all in your mouth quickly?

3 ?

Two children are throwing stones at a window.

Do you:

1 Join in and throw stones too?

2 Go and tell the owner?

3 ?

You have promised to help the Church group to clear away some rubbish. Your friend asks you to play with him instead.
Do you:
1 Phone the leader to say you are ill?
2 Go, and grumble all the time?
3 ?

You are playing a game with your friend and he/she is winning.
Do you:
1 Cheat?
2 Pretend you are ill and give up?
3 ?

A big boy dares you to break into the school. He says you are a baby if you don't.
Do you:
1 Do as he says?
2 Run and tell your teacher?
3 ?

You badly want a new computer game/toy but you have been told you cannot have it and you do not have enough pocket money to buy it yourself.
Do you:
1 Steal money from your parents?
2 Keep complaining to your Mum until she gives in?
3 ?

Your friend says that Church is boring.
Do you:
1 Believe him and refuse to go?
2 Make excuses not to go?
3 ?

An old lady has given you a present that is far too young for you. She is very old and poor and some people think she is silly.
Do you:
1 Throw the present back at her?
2 Tell her she is stupid?
3 ?

A gang wants you to join them, but to do so you have to fight with one of the little children/break friends with all your other friends.
Do you:
1 Do what the gang says?
2 Fight the gang leader instead?
3 ?

Your sister/brother/friend has some new shoes when he/she grows out of his/hers.
Do you:
1 Complain because you haven't got some?
2 Deliberately kick mud all over his/her shoes?
3 ?

Build a church

The Christian Church is made up of people who are Christians. They try to follow what Jesus taught. Christians are not always good. Like everybody else, Christians get it wrong sometimes. Even when we get it wrong, God will always forgive us. Think of some Christians that you know. How can others tell that we are trying to follow Jesus? What do we do that shows we are Christians?

Build a church out of cardboard boxes. Try to make it like your own church if possible. On some of the bricks or stones you can draw the people of the church and the ways in which they try

Reading the Bible

Most Christians read their Bibles regularly to help them learn more about God and how Jesus lived on this earth. Do you have a Bible? You could try to read a little part of your Bible every day. There are so many interesting and exciting stories. (See more in session 9, The Bible.)

PRAYER AND PRAISE

Prayer bricks

Use the largest play bricks or simply make card bricks that can be pasted onto the wall. (If you are using play bricks you will need to write on paper and attach the paper to the bricks.) Write or draw on your bricks the kinds of things that Christians do to try and follow Jesus. Think of the people that go to your church. What do they do that shows that they are Christians?

Build up your bricks to make a Church. As you place the brick on the wall, you can offer a prayer of thanks for all those who try to follow Jesus by doing these things, however small they may seem.

to be good Christians. Why do you think they are Christians? What qualities do they have? For example:

- Old Mrs Jones who always has a smile and a kind word for everybody
- Mr Smith who visits people who are ill
- Miss Brown who helps the children in Sunday club

319 **Christ be my leader**
363 **His name was Saul**
364 **His ways are not our ways**
367 **I am the Church**
426 **M-m-m-m-must I really go**
442 **On the road to Damascus**
487 **We're following Jesus**
492 **What made a difference**

Five

BAPTISM

INTRODUCTION

People who want to follow Jesus Christ are called Christians. That does not mean that they are very good people although they do try to be. Anybody can be a Christian. It does not matter whether we are fat or thin, tall or short, black or white, dark or fair, clever or not. God is happy to have us in his family whatever we are like.

Many people like to share their joy in this message with others who feel the same. They want to worship God together. Those who want to follow Christ in this way are called the Church. This is not the building but the people. There are millions across the world who make up the Church of God. People join together in groups and these groups often go to praise God in buildings called churches. We don't have to go to church to worship God, but many people find it helps to have others around them who will help them to learn more about God. There are many different kinds of churches, with people who have different ideas on how to worship and work for God. The differences are not important as long as we remember the really important thing. *We are all children of God.*

You may go to any church and be welcome there, but how do you become a member of the Church? Most people like to feel that they belong. When a person is baptized, he or she becomes a member, is taken into the family of the Church. We can be baptized at any age. In some churches, members are often baptized as babies or young children. In other churches, baptism marks the time when Christians are old enough to decide for themselves that they want to follow Jesus and they declare this in front of witnesses.

Have you been baptized? You may have been too young to remember what happened. If you were baptized as a baby, try and find out:

- The date of your baptism: _____
- Did you wear special clothes for your baptism?
- Have you got the card that you were given when you were baptized?

If you were baptized as a baby, this, or something like it, is what will have happened:

Duties of parents and godparents

When we are very young, we need help with many things. Your parents and godparents promised to help you learn about God, to learn to pray and to go to church. In front of the whole congregation, your godparents made those promises for you.

Your godparents are:

_____

_____

The sign of the cross
The person who baptized you made the sign of the cross on your forehead. Why was the sign of the cross used?

Water
The minister (whoever baptized you) blessed some water to make it special. Then he poured a little water over your head and said: 'I baptize you in the name of the Father, and of the Son, and of the Holy Spirit.'

We use water to wash. The minister used the water to show that we wash away, or put aside, anything that is bad in us and leave only the good parts. The water is a symbol.

The lighted candle
We tend to connect 'darkness' with bad things and 'light' with good things. Jesus said that he was the 'Light of the world'. When we decide to follow Jesus we want only good. The minister may have given you a lighted candle to show you that as a member of the Church, you will try to follow Jesus' good ways. The candle, like the water, is a symbol. Do you still have that candle? Do you ever light it to remind you of your baptism?

The welcome
The whole congregation (other members of the Church) may have greeted you and welcomed you as a member of the Church.

You may have a chance to watch a baptism. If there are no baptisms due in the church, ask your priest or minister to show you what he or she does when he baptizes somebody. What is the name of the place where baptism takes place?

Christians have copied the idea of baptism from events of Jesus' own life. Most Christian baptism is a mixture of the baptism of Jesus by John and the presentation of the baby Jesus in the Temple.

STORY

John baptizes Jesus
Matthew 3:13–17
The wild man of the desert (p. 140)

Read the story of the baptism of Jesus. What do you know about John the Baptist? Write a description, or draw a picture of him. Where was Jesus baptized? What happened? Use your own words to tell a friend the story.

Jesus was not baptized as a baby but he was taken to the Temple in Jerusalem. That is celebrated at Candlemas. The story is found in Luke 2:21–40 (see session 15).

ACTIVITIES

Pretend baptism

Use a doll to hold a baptism. You will need to choose parents and godparents for the baby and perhaps a minister. You could dress up in your best clothes as the real parents and godparents would. You will need water and a candle. You may even bake a cake to have after the ceremony. Remember the promises made on behalf of the baby, the sign of the cross on the baby's forehead, and the welcome by all the rest of the Church family.

What do Christians believe? — scroll

Most Christians would find it quite difficult to explain exactly what they believe about God. A long time ago, the leaders of the Church realized this. They thought very hard and wrote a short statement that told what Christians believe. This statement of belief is called a *Creed*. (This happened more than once so there are several creeds, but they say very much the same thing.)

A simple form of the Creed is often used in a baptism service. Basically Christians believe that:

- God is the Creator (sometimes called Father) and he made the world and gave it life.
- Jesus is the Son of God, who lived on earth as a man. His life was a pattern for us to try to follow. He died for us but is alive again.
- The Spirit of God lives in us to help us to know God better and to love others.

You will need:
- *paper (cartridge paper if possible)*
- *felt pen*
- *tea bag*
- *broom handle*
- *ribbon*

Prepare the paper first. A good quality paper will help. Rub it with a damp tea bag. This will make it discoloured. Carefully tear the edges — not too much — just to make it look old. Gently wrap the paper around the broom handle and leave to dry. You will need to open it out carefully. Write what Christians believe on your paper. You could make your scroll look really special by tying a ribbon round it.

Promise biscuits

If you have a kitchen nearby, you could make some biscuits, but a packet of plain biscuits will do just as well. You will need some icing in a bag or tube with a fine nozzle. (These can be bought in tubes already mixed.)

Think of what the godparents promise for the baby at a baptism. Use the icing to write on the biscuits what you promise in trying to follow Jesus.

PRAYER AND PRAISE

Let us recall what Christians believe and the promises made for us at baptism.

Leader   Do you believe and trust in God the Creator, who made the world and loves all that he made?

All   **I believe and trust in him.**

Leader   Do you believe and trust in Jesus, the Son of God, who lived to show us how to live and died for us, but is now alive?

All   **I believe and trust in him.**

Leader   Do you believe and trust in the Holy Spirit, who lives in us to help us know God better and to help us love others more?

All   **I believe and trust in him.**

Leader   This is what Christians all over the world believe.

All   **This is what we believe.**

Help us to live our lives like Jesus and tell others of God's love for all.

Leader   We pray that we may remember these things and act on them at all times.

All   **We promise before God that we will do our best to follow his ways. Amen.**

  42 **Father, I place into your hands**
  98 **I have decided to follow Jesus**
122 **I want to live for Jesus ev'ry day**
124 **I want to walk with Jesus Christ**
138 **Jesus I will come with you**
186 **On Jordan's bank the Baptist's cry**
367 **I am the Church!**
383 **I've come to a time**

Six

ALL SAINTS

INTRODUCTION

What is a saint? How are saints different from you and me? Think of some of the saints you may have heard of. What do you notice about them that makes them saints? Do you remember St Francis, for instance? When he came to know Jesus his life changed.

All Saints Day is the day when we celebrate the lives of saints through the ages. On 1 November every year the Church sets aside a day to remember All Saints. These are not just for the well known saints, such as the first followers of Jesus. They have their own days on which we remember them especially. All Saints Day is also for the hundreds of people who have no special day of their own but have tried so hard to do what Jesus told us to do. Most of them were not extra special people in the eyes of others, but to God they were *very* special.

STORY

There is a lady who has lived most of her life in India. She is an old lady, quite small and thin, and she owns very little. Hardly anybody knows her real name. Nevertheless, this lady has become very well-known in the world and many people, including the rich and the famous, travel long distances to meet

and talk with her. She is *not* offically a saint but they, along with most people who have heard about this lady, consider that she is very much like a saint. You may have heard of her. She is called Mother Teresa.

What do you know about Mother Teresa? There are many accounts of the life of Mother Teresa of Calcutta. The following is a brief summary of her story:

The woman we have come to know as Mother Teresa was born just before World War I in what was Yugoslavia.

She was called Agnes. From the beginning she wanted to work for Jesus. When she heard about the work of some nuns in India, Agnes felt that this was what God wanted her to do.

At the age of eighteen Agnes went first to Ireland and then to Darjeeling in India where she learned how to be a nun and trained as a teacher — a teacher of geography. When she took her vows, made her promises, to become a nun Agnes took on the name of Teresa and became Sister Teresa. She went to teach in a large, mainly poor city on the banks of the great River Ganges in the north-east of India. This was Calcutta. For twenty years Sister Teresa taught teenage girls geography.

Gradually, Teresa became aware of the dreadful poverty in Calcutta. She saw hundreds of sick and homeless lying in the streets, with nowhere to live, nobody to care for them. Many were starving and sick with a terrible disease called leprosy. Many had no clothes or even a blanket to keep them warm on the cold nights lying on the streets. Teresa was so sad. She knew that God didn't want his children to live like this. Many of them died with nobody to care for them.

She knew that it was no use just being sad. She must *do* something about these poor people. Jesus had told the story about how people had helped others and in doing so had helped him. Teresa gave up teaching and did a quick course in nursing. These people couldn't learn; most of them were too sick to do anything. Most of them would die soon but at least Teresa would make their last days as comfortable and happy as possible.

The nuns with whom she had worked were a teaching Order. She had to ask permission to leave that Order and set up a new group of nursing nuns. This became called the Missionaries of Charity. She opened a home for the dying in an old, disused church. Some of the girls who had been taught by Teresa in the past gave Mother Teresa (as she had now become) money for medicine and all the other things these sick people needed.

The home was soon filled. Mothers who couldn't feed their babies would even leave them in dustbins, knowing that Mother Teresa and her nuns would find them and look after them. The work grew and grew. More and more people, many of them former pupils of Teresa, asked to join the Missionaries of Charity. Their work began to spread right across India. The work was hard and often very sad. The sisters gave love and care to everybody.

This is not 'A long time ago . . .' story: the work goes on now. There are still thousands of poor and sick people who need the help of those sisters, and now there is an Order of monks — The Brothers of Charity — to help the nuns.

Mother Teresa believes that 'each person is a child of God and resembles God. So each person deserves care and love.' Do you think Mother Teresa is like a saint? What qualities make Mother Teresa like a saint?

ACTIVITIES

Remembering quiz
Find the answers to these (and other) questions:

- What was Teresa's name?
- Where was she born?
- Where did she first go for training?
- What is the name of the great city where she taught?

- What is the name of the river on which this city stands?
- What did Teresa teach?
- How many years did she teach?
- What is the terrible disease that killed many of the people on the streets?
- What is the name of the new Order of nuns?
- What training did Teresa do to help her help the street people?
- Where did mothers leave the babies they could not feed?
- Who gave money to help Teresa in her work?
- What does Mother Teresa believe that makes her do this work?

Your own wordsearch

You will need:
- *squared paper and pencil*
- *words connected with the saint's story*

Choose words that are important to the story of Mother Teresa (like some of the answers to the Remembering quiz). Make a big box square — about 20 X 20 squares. Write the words inside the box — each of the letters of the words in one of the little squares. The words may go across or down like in a crossword. Sometimes a letter from one word may be the same as from another:

<pre>
        A
        G
   I N D I A
        E
        S
</pre>

When all the words are in place, fill in the left-over spaces with other letters. They should not be in any particular order or spell any other words.

List the words you have used under the wordsearch. Get your friends to try your wordsearch. They should put a line through each word as they find it and cross off that word on the list.

The backing paper of sticky-back plastic is often printed with squares and is useful if you are making a big wordsearch for quite a large group to see. When you finish, if you cover your wordsearch with the sticky-back plastic, wrong answers may be rubbed out and the right ones inserted instead as long as only water-based felt pens are used.

Saints wheel

There are many 'minor' saints recorded in many books. Most of them have a particular sign/symbol and these are often shown in the books of their lives. You will need these signs and symbols or pictures, as well as the date on which the saint is remembered.

Cut out a large circle from stiff card. Divide the circle into twelve sections and head each section with the name of a calendar month. In each section write the name and draw the symbol or a picture of a saint who is remembered during that month.

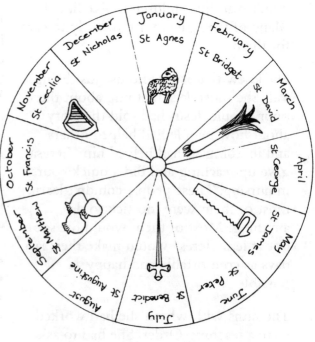

Saints calendar

Use a calendar that has each day in a square of its own. Pin the sheets of each month onto a stiff piece of card but *do not stick* them on yet. Make 'doors' from the dates on which saints are remembered, e.g. 4 October — St Francis. In the space under that date, draw the saint's symbol or picture and write his/her name. When all the saints' days are in place stick the month sheet over the top, making sure that you can still open the 'doors' to reveal the saints.

Saints Snap Game

You will need:
- *at least 24 small cards, all the same size*
- *a book of saints with pictures and symbols*
- *crayons/felt pens*

Copy pictures of saints and/or write their names onto cards. Copy the symbols of those saints onto other cards. Match the symbol to the name/picture. You could make other cards with pictures of things that happened to the saints for which they are remembered.

All Saints banner

Make a banner showing the exploits of as many saints as you can remember.

Instead of pictures of these saints you could use their own particular symbols. See session 30 for instructions.

PRAYER AND PRAISE

For all the saints (found in most regular hymn books)

115 **I sing a song of the saints**
195 **O when the saints**

389 **If you want to be great**
392 **I'm going to shine, shine, shine**

Seven

PATRON SAINTS

INTRODUCTION

Three of the Patron Saints of the British Isles are remembered within a few weeks of each other:

> St David (Patron Saint of Wales)—
> 1 March
> St Patrick (Patron Saint of Ireland) —
> 17 March
> St George (Patron Saint of England)
> — 23 April

The other Patron Saint (Scotland) is St Andrew — 30 November.

What is a Patron Saint? 'Patron' comes from the Latin word *Pater*, which means Father. Like a Father, the Patron protects, encourages and supports. Many people believe that their Patron Saint will speak to God on their behalf — a kind of go-between. Many people adopt their own saint — one who's life and character reflects their own. Groups of people who shared the same job often clubbed together and prayed to the Patron Saint for their trade or art. Can you think of a saint who was a carpenter?★

Children have a Patron Saint — a bishop who lived a long time ago in Myra — St Nicholas. He was said to have saved the

lives of some children threatened with a terrible death. If you were to choose a Patron Saint for yourself, which one would you choose? What special attributes would that saint need?

Churches sometimes have a Patron Saint. What is the name of your church? Is that the church's Patron Saint? Could you think of a more appropriate, better suited, saint for your church?

STORY

Read or tell the story of your own Patron Saint, or, if the church is not dedicated to a saint, choose one of particular interest. Many of the stories are based purely on legend and bear little relation to fact. Think particularly of why the saint behaved as he or she did in trying to follow Jesus.

One of the following may be used. They are the stories of the Patron Saints of Great Britain.

ST ANDREW —
30 November

Andrew brings his brother to Jesus John 1:37—41

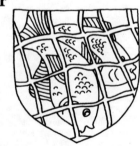

★ St Joseph was chosen as the Patron Saint of carpenters because he was a carpenter himself.

ACTIVITIES

Fisherman Andrew and his boat

Make a boat out of large cartons. A cardboard tube (used to hold fabric) or a broom handle makes a good mast for the boat. Sails can be made from old sheets. Hang a piece of netting over the side of the boat (netting is usually available from garden centres, sold as fruit netting). Make fish from painted paper or card. Cut out and tangle them amongst the threads of the nets. Make at least two figures — Andrew and his brother — to pull in the nets. Figures may be easily made from:

- a paper plate (the face)
- a garden cane (the body)
- a wire coat hanger, squashed flat and wound round the cane (the arms)
- wrapped in an old sheet or large piece of scrap material (the clothing)

St Andrew — This is Your Life

Look up as much information as you can about St Andrew. The Bible, Bible encyclopaedias and handbooks should give you some information. Use this information, as well as your imagination, to create a *This is Your Life* programme on St Andrew, like the one on television. You might interview Peter, his brother; other disciples like Philip or James and John; and perhaps the little boy who gave Andrew his lunch to share with Jesus. Remember that Andrew is often known as the first missionary because it was St Andrew that called his brother, Simon Peter, to come and join Jesus.

Don't forget to paint a large picture of Andrew, and perhaps his boat, to hang behind the people as they speak.

You could use the figures suggested for the first activity instead of people if you are shy. The puppets could speak the words of the characters.

This activity can be done for any of the saints.

ST DAVID — 1 March

David is the Patron Saint of Wales. In Welsh his name is 'Dewi Sant'. He lived in the sixth century. He was greatly loved by the Welsh people when he lived among them. He was known as a great preacher and friend. It is said that David preached to thousands of people in a valley in Dyfed. (You may still hear it referred to as Cardiganshire.) There were many bishops listening to him too and they were worried that such a vast number of people would not be able to hear him. According to the legend, as David spoke, the ground under his feet rose up until it became a mountain. Everybody could see and hear David. Afterwards a church was built there and dedicated to St David.

The daffodil and leek are associated with him: they can be seen on coins and stamps of Wales. One story tells how St David was called on to help his people fight an intruding army in a narrow valley. The people from both sides were dressed alike. The only way they could identify the enemy was by David's men picking leeks from a field and sticking then in their helmets. Now, soldiers in the Welsh regiments wear a leek on St

David's Day. Another story is that David ate such simple food, mainly bread and leeks, and was such a wonderful preacher that the people thought that the leeks may help them to be as good as David.

Little else is known about him other than that he was the first bishop in those parts and founded a monastery in Pembrokeshire (another part of Dyfed). The monks were called 'watermen' because they were not allowed to drink wine and only drank water. He died around 589.

There is a cathedral in Wales named after him and it is still there, used for regular services and visited by hundreds of people each year. The small town where it was built is also called St David's.

ACTIVITY

St David's 'four Ps' cross

The life of St David was based on 'four Ps' — Prayer, Praise, Poverty and Preaching. St David may well have preached at a cross that would have been placed in the centre of the village. Build a cross from boxes and cartons. Decorate it with Celtic designs. On the front of the four boxes that form the vertical part of the cross put pictures of the saint representing each of the four Ps.

ST PATRICK — 17 March

There are many stories told about Patrick. He was born a very long time ago — about 1,600 years ago! When he was only a teenager he was captured by pirates and taken to Ireland. Soon he grew to love the country, but he knew that he had to escape or he would be a prisoner all his life. At last he managed to escape and sailed to what is now called France.

He studied hard to become a priest. Only when he had learned enough did he return to the beautiful land of Ireland.

He made his way to Tara, the home of Loaghaire, the chief King. The King had ordered that no fire should be lit, on penalty of death. Patrick was determined to break the power of the wizards who had advised the King. As long as they were so powerful, the King would not listen to Patrick. Patrick lit a huge bonfire and everybody was frightened. They knew that the King would be furious at being disobeyed. Immediately, Patrick was arrested and taken before the King. Patrick was not afraid. He told the King that he had deliberately lit the fire so that he could speak with him. The King was impressed by Patrick's courage: 'Since you are not afraid, you may speak.'

Patrick started to tell the King his story. The King knew nothing about Jesus, so Patrick told Loaghaire the wonderful story of Jesus: how he loved so much that he became a man on earth; how he taught his disciples and cured those who were sick; how he died a cruel death to save us. King Loaghaire was so interested in the story that he asked Patrick to stay with him. The King became a Christian and often had long discussions with Patrick.

One day, the King asked Patrick about this strange thing called the 'Trinity'. How can there be just one God, but God the Father, God the Son and God the Holy Spirit? That sounded more like three Gods! Patrick looked at the ground where there grew a small, three-leaved plant called a shamrock. 'Look at the leaf of the shamrock,' he said. 'It has three parts to the leaf and yet it is only one leaf. In the same way, God has three forms, yet is *one* God.' Much later, Patrick's words were remembered and the shamrock was adopted as the special symbol of Ireland.

Patrick is now remembered as the special, or Patron Saint of Ireland. The hymn 'St Patrick's Breastplate' is supposed to have been written by him.

ACTIVITY

St Patrick's shamrock

St Patrick explained how the Trinity is like the shamrock. The shamrock is very much like clover. There are three separate parts to the shamrock leaf and yet it is one leaf. In the same way there are three different, separate parts to the Trinity — God the Father, God the Son and God the Holy Spirit. Together they make one God.

Make a great big shamrock from green paper or card (this can be painted). You could draw some of the events of Patrick's life on the shamrock leaf.

ST GEORGE — 23 April

St George has been the Patron Saint of England since the fourteenth century, but he actually never came near England as far as we know. He was born in the third century in the country now called Turkey. His parents were Christians. He became a soldier of high rank in the Roman army and was said to be a courageous, polite and handsome man. He became upset that the Roman emperor was persecuting Christians and felt that he could not stay in the Roman army any longer. So he sold his possessions, gave up his position and went to see the emperor. When the emperor heard George was a Christian he had him tortured and beheaded. George was buried near the coast at Lydda with other persecuted Christians. These are the only facts known about George but many legends have grown up around him.

The most famous story about St George is the one where he meets the dragon. A dragon kept the whole country in terror as it poisoned with its breath everybody who came near. Every day it demanded an offering of two sheep as food to stop it from killing humans. At last the people ran out of sheep. They drew lots to choose who should go as the dragon's victim. The King's daughter drew the straw. Everybody was so sad, but the Princess was determined to go. When George heard what was about to happen he hurried to the place. With his lance he pierced the dragon and killed it. (Another story says that he didn't kill the dragon, but tied a rope round it's neck and led it back to the city as tame as any pet.)

George told the people not to be afraid. If they would believe in Jesus and be baptized, they need never be afraid again. Hundreds of the people were baptized that day. George would take no reward for himself. Instead, the King and all his people built churches and helped poor people. Whether you believe there were ever such creatures as dragons or not doesn't matter. George may have been able to rid the country of some local 'pest' but more importantly he was able to tell the people all about Jesus. Much later, people remembered the good man who believed so firmly in the power of Jesus and they called him a saint.

His flag is a red cross on a white background. Sometimes you can see this flag flying on its own, or as part of the Union Jack.

ACTIVITY

St George and the dragon

This is such a good story to act out. Create the dragon from bags and boxes and perhaps an old sheet or blanket. Do ensure that you remember: *never to put plastic or polythene bags over your face.*

Remember that St George's dragon represents all that is bad and evil in the world. We are urged to be like George and fight all this evil ourselves. The dragon could be decorated with symbols of those bad and evil things: symbols or pictures of war, famine, drugs and crime.

George himself can wear armour made from boxes covered in silver foil, or a silver coloured tunic (painted with silver paint.) Use a cardboard box for his helmet. Don't forget the shield which could have on it St George's cross — the red cross on a white background. Symbols and pictures of good and peace could be used to decorate St George's armour.

PRAYER AND PRAISE

Lord, thank you for those who have known you and wanted to share that knowledge of your love with others. Thank you especially for Saint ———, who is our Patron Saint. Help us to be more like him/her and to live our lives as you want us to. Amen.

115 I sing a song of the saints
195 O when the saints

. . .

REMEMBRANCE SUNDAY

INTRODUCTION

On Remembrance Sunday you will see lots of parades of soldiers or ex-soldiers, most of them wearing rows of medals on their chests and almost certainly wearing red poppies. There will be special services in many churches to remember those who died in battle. We remember with honour and thanks those who died whilst fighting to save our country and all its people from great danger.

Britain has had many wars in its history but usually on Remembrance Sunday we think of the soldiers who died in the First and Second World Wars (1914–1918) and (1939–1945). Thousands of mainly young men died, fighting for their country. Now we remember, too, the Falklands War and the Gulf War, plus the 'war' that continues in and around Ireland.

War is terrible. Whatever you have seen on films and television, war is not funny (although no doubt people had funny experiences even amongst the horror). People are hurt, often very badly. People are killed. Families are split up. Homes and lives are ruined.

STORY

Love one another
Luke 6:27–38

Is war ever right?
All through the ages humans have fought each other. Think why armies have marched to defeat others:

- invasion or threat of invasion from another country
- the leader wanting more power and land
- defence of a country threatened by another country
- essential resources cut off by another country

There are many who say that God will

fight with them — be on their side —
because they fight for right. Many
psalms imply this (e.g. Psalm 7). Also
many Bible stories — particularly in the
Old Testament — tell of war and killing,
and how God (according to the writers)
helped them to win.

There are many who say that we should
never fight. Jesus said: 'Do not take
revenge on someone who wrongs you.
If anyone slaps you on the right cheek,
let him slap your left cheek too,'
(Matthew 5:39) and 'Love your enemies
and pray for those who persecute you.'
(Matthew 5:44) Does this mean that we
should never fight at all?

Should we fight to protect the
oppressed — people who are poor and
need protection and help? Should we
stand by and let a brutal leader send in
his army to kill defenceless people?
Should we fight for *right?* Who knows
what is right?

You may be a very gentle, peaceful
person, or you may be naturally rather
aggressive (perhaps you rather like a
fight!). What would make *you* fight?

- invasion or threat of invasion by
  another country?
- somebody threatening your family or
  friends?
- somebody attacking you personally?
- wanting more power and land
  yourself?
- somebody calling you names?

ACTIVITIES

War memorial
Design and make a large war memorial
— either just painted on to a board or
from boxes stacked and stuck together,
then painted like stone. Decide together
what message you would want to give

to people who see your memorial,
about war and the way to peace. Write
or paint this carefully on the memorial.

Think what flower would symbolize
peace. You could make your own
flower, the yellow rose called 'Peace', or
the traditional poppy. Surround the
memorial with wreaths of the flowers.
Prayers could be written and placed in
the middle of the wreaths.

Soldiers remembered at the memorial
are often marked by small wooden
crosses on which are written their
names. Instead, the names of countries
where there is war and fighting could
be written on crosses (made from
lollipop sticks, garden tags or simply
strips of card) and placed around the
memorial.

Poppy prayers
Poppies have been made by ex-
servicemen for many years to remind
people about the horrors of war. They
remind us that thousands of soldiers and
civilians died in war, and that we must
work together to make sure that never

again should war be allowed to kill thousands and ruin the lives of even more.

And yet, at this minute, somewhere in the world, soldiers will be killing other soldiers. One group of people will be at war with another. Think what we can do to try to prevent more war.

Write prayers for peace and understanding amongst all nations. Cut out poppies from paper – just four petals, and probably about 20 cm.

across would be enough. Stick your prayer on the poppy. Arrange all the poppies on a board together. You could write the names of places where there is war and fighting, each on a little wooden cross, and place them amongst the poppies.

PRAYER AND PRAISE

Lord, it is easy to say 'Let there be peace on earth', but as long as I hold thoughts of revenge and aggression, as long as I quarrel and fight, the world will be like me. Soldiers will die and their families will suffer. Help me to begin to make the world a place of peace and love. Amen.

  81 **Hévénu shalom aléchem**
161 **Make me a channel of your peace**
196 **Peace, I give to you**
202 **Praise him, praise him**
425 **Love, joy, peace**

Nine

THE BIBLE

INTRODUCTION

The Bible is an amazing book. It is not just one book but a series of books written by many different people. All those people felt close to God and knew that they must pass on to others all the faith and knowledge that they possessed.

There are two parts to the Bible — the Old and the New Testament. The Old Testament deals with the time before the birth of Jesus — the lives and teaching of the people of Israel. The New Testament tells of the life of Jesus on this earth and the effect this had on others. In some Bibles you will find the two parts are linked by the Apocrypha. The Bible contains many exciting stories that tell of the adventures of God's special people, the Israelites. Some of the stories are funny, some are sad, many are truly wonderful. As well as the historical events in the lives of the Israelites, there are books that give the law by which these Israelites were told they must live. There are books of poetry and songs. There are letters written by Christian leaders to new Christians who needed guidance and help on how they should live their lives as good Christians.

The Bible is a whole library of books with something for everybody. It is really worth reading.

Can you find a part of the Bible that gives some 'Do it yourself' instructions?★

ACTIVITIES

Your own Bible library
You will need:
- *a Bible*
- *sheets of white paper*
- *sheets of card (assorted colours)*
- *crayons/felt pens*
- *wool or thread and needle*
- *box*
- *sticky-back plastic, wallpaper or wrapping paper*

Fold one sheet of paper inside a sheet of card like a thin book. Repeat this for every book of the Bible. Stitch each book together at the fold. Write the names of the books on the outer covers. Design your cover with an appropriate picture or design. For each book of the Bible decide the essential content — story/message of that book. Either write this or illustrate it with a picture/series of pictures on the inside sheet of each book. There are four sides to the folded sheet, so use them all if necessary. The cover cards could be colour-coded to show the different types of content they represent:-

★ Answer: Genesis — Noah is told how to make an ark.

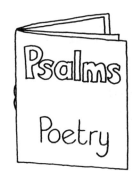

- green   The Prophets
                 Isaiah to Malachi
- blue   New Testament History
                 Matthew to Acts
- purple   The Letters
                 Romans to Jude
- black   Revelation

Find a suitable box into which the books may fit. 'Micro' washing powder boxes are strong and a useful size — wipe out all residual powder before use. Cover the box with sticky-back plastic, wallpaper or wrapping paper. Stand the 'books' in the box to keep them together.

Bible time line
You will need:
- *a Bible*
- *a roll of plain wallpaper or similar*
- *crayons/felt pens*
- *Blu-tack*

The roll of paper will need to stretch as far around the room/church as you can

- red   The Book of the Law
               (Torah)
                 Genesis to
                 Deuteronomy
- orange   Old Testament History
                 Joshua to Esther
- yellow   Poetry and Wisdom
                 Job to Song of Songs

manage. Where there is no room for the time line to go round the building, the roll may be folded, zig-zag, and opened up only for inspection.

Identify the key events/teachings in the Bible story. (See the list following for examples.) You may like to tell each of the stories in your own words with appropriate illustrations, or simply draw pictures, perhaps with a caption, to explain more clearly the event portrayed.

It may be easier to make two time lines — an Old Testament edition and a New Testament one. If it is left as one long line, find a point about two thirds of the way along to mark as the birth of Jesus. Place the stories and special teachings in order along the line. It may be easier to stick the pictures to the paper with Blu-tack until you are sure of the sequence.

Some or all of the following could be used:

The Old Testament
The Creation
The Fall
Noah and the Flood
Tower of Babel
Abraham
Isaac
Twelve sons of Jacob
Israelite slaves
Baby Moses
Escape from Egypt
Ten Commandments
Joshua in Jericho
Deborah
Gideon
Samson
Ruth
Samuel
Saul is made King
David and Goliath
King David
King Solomon and the Temple

The divided Kingdom
Elijah and prophets of Baal
Jezebel
Elisha
Israel conquered
Exile to Babylon
Daniel
Return to Jerusalem
Jonah
Esther
Psalms

Apocrypha
Maccabees
Roman conquest

This project will take time to accomplish so it could become an 'on-going' activity to which contributions are added over a long period of time.

The New Testament
John the Baptist born
Annunciation
Birth of Jesus
Boy Jesus in the Temple
John the Baptist
The temptations
The twelve disciples
Stories told by Jesus
Miracles
Teaching — Lord's Prayer
Sermon on the Mount
Palm Sunday
Last Supper
Trial of Jesus
Crucifixion
Resurrection
Ascension
Pentecost
Stephen
Peter and John in prison
Paul — Road to Damascus
Paul's journeys
Paul shipwrecked
Letters — The Body of Christ
Peter — vision on the roof
Revelation

PRAYER AND PRAISE

Leader   You have given us your Word
in the Bible.
Listen to his Word.

All   **Great is your Word.
Great is your love.**

Leader   You have told us of your love
for us.
Experience his love.

All   **Great is your name.
Great is your love.**

Leader   You have created all things.
Share in his Creation.

All   **Great is your Creation.
Great is your love.**

Leader   Through the example of Jesus
we have learned how to live.
Follow his Way.

All   **Great is the Way.
Great is your love.**

Leader   You died for us on a cruel
cross.

All   **Great, so great is your love.**

Leader   You rose again and live with
us.

All   **Alleluia!**

*The collect for Advent 2 is suitable for use
here.*

163   **Make the Book live to me**
227   **Tell me the old, old story**
228   **Tell me the stories of Jesus**
234   **The best book to read is the
Bible**
458   **Six hundred years old was the
preacher**

Ten

HANUKAH

INTRODUCTION

In John 10:22 you will read that Jesus was in Jerusalem during the Feast of Dedication, and that it was winter. Another name for this festival is *Hanukah*. As well as having other names for the Jewish festival of Hanukah the spelling of that name is often different too. It is sometimes spelled Hanukkah, Chanuka or Chanukkah.

All through their history, the people of Israel have suffered attacks from enemies. The main reason for the constant attacks was because of their strategic position. They lived on a kind of crossroads, where trade routes met — on the edge of the Mediterranean Sea — linking Europe, Africa and Asia. From the time that they settled in the Promised Land, every time they forgot their special relationship with God, enemies would come along and conquer them.

STORY

Judas Maccabeus

About 200 years before Jesus was born, the kingdoms of Israel and Judah were troubled with many enemies. King *Antiochus* of *Syria*, which was part of the great *Greek* empire, had conquered the Jews and forced them to obey his laws

rather than the laws given to them by God. King Antiochus thought that he was a god himself, the God *Zeus*. He had statues made of himself and ordered that everybody should bow down and worship the statues. One of the ten great Commandments given by God is: 'Do not bow down to any statue and worship it.' Many Jews refused to obey the King's orders and were quickly put to death.

In a small town called *Modin*, north-west of Jerusalem, there lived a *priest* called *Mattathias*. When soldiers came to the town to enforce the King's orders, Mattathias bravely refused to bow down and worship the statue of Zeus. He even killed the *captain* of the army who tried to make the people follow the King's laws. Mattathias and his family had to escape into the hills of the Judean wilderness. From there Mattathias led his followers in a *rebellion*. Groups would creep out and attack the Syrian soldiers when they were least expecting them. This small guerilla force, or freedom fighters, began to grow as the Jews learned how they were defeating their enemies but they were still only a few against a very powerful enemy. Eventually, after many hard battles, the old priest died and his son, *Judas*, took over as leader.

Judas was so successful against the

Syrian army that he earned himself the nickname *Maccabeus* (this is sometimes written *Maccabees*). This means '*hammerer*' because he 'hammered' the enemy. In spite of being such a small group, at last they were able to defeat the Syrian army. Judas and his guerillas marched into their holy city, Jerusalem. Immediately they went to the most important place in the city, the *Temple*. There they had hoped to say thank you to God for their victory. However a dreadful sight met their eyes. The Temple was filled with statues of Zeus and other gods and the air was filled with the smell of sacrificed pigs. Pigs are considered unclean to the Jews!

The Temple had to be cleansed from top to bottom and *re-dedicated* to the worship of the one and only God. There was a great lamp holder, called a *menorah*, in the Temple. It had seven lamps that were supposed to be kept lit day and night. The oil that was used for the lamps was special. It had to go through a long process of blessing and purification. Judas and his men found only enough *sacred oil* to light the menorah for one day and it needed several days to prepare more oil. Nevertheless, they lit the menorah and got on with the work of cleansing the Temple. This was when a 'great miracle happened there'. The lamp burned for *eight* days!

The Jewish feast of Hanukah remembers the time of Judas, the 'great miracle' of the burning lamps, and how the Temple was re-dedicated to the worship of God.

Jesus would have known the story and would have celebrated the Feast, as Jews do today (see John 10:22). Other names for the Feast are the Festival of Lights or Re-Dedication. Jews re-dedicate themselves at this time. They ask forgiveness for all that they have done wrong over the past year and promise to try to do better in the following year.

Each home will have a special Hanukah menorah, called a Hanukiyah. These usually hold candles rather than oil lamps now. Instead of seven lights as are found in the ordinary menorah, there are nine on the Hanukiyah — eight for each day that the Temple menorah remained lit, and another 'servant' candle or *shamash* from which all the other candles are lit.

ACTIVITIES

Fill in the word

Having heard the story through, the following words could be written on separate cards and held up by the children at the appropriate places in the story as it is retold. Alternatively, the story could be written out with gaps for the words (found in italic type). Try to put the words in the right places in the story.

sacred oil	Maccabeus	Zeus
Greek	Modin	rebellion
Syria	Judas	hammerer
menorah	Antiochus	Mattathias
re-dedicated	shamash	eight
priest	Temple	captain

Hanukah crossword

Across

3. A seven-branched lamp (7)
4. Freedom fighters (9)
5. The number of days that the lamp remained lit (5)
11. Sacred _ _ _ was used to light the lamp in the Temple (3)
12. The Temple had to be _ _ _ after the Syrians left (2-9)
14. The nickname of Judas (9)
15. Syria was part of this empire (5)
16. A great _ _ _ happened there (7)
17. The 'servant' candle (7)
19. Mattathias was one of these (6)
20. Mattathias killed a _ _ _ of the Syrian army (7)
22. The Jewish festival which celebrates this story (7)

Down

1. The old priest's name (10)
2. The most holy place in Jerusalem (6)
6. Part of the Greek empire (5)
7. The Syrian king's name (9)
8. The name of the old priest's son (5)
9. An armed resistance against authority (9)
10. The meaning of the nickname given to Judas (8)
13. The place in Judea where Mattathias' soldiers hid (10)
18. The town where the old priest lived (5)
21. A large group of soldiers (4)

Answers are at the end of the book.

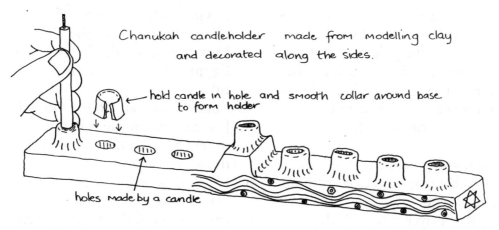

Chanukah candleholder made from modelling clay and decorated along the sides.

← hold candle in hole and smooth collar around base to form holder

holes made by a candle

the eight candles are to be at the same height with the shamash or servant candle, which lights the others, higher.

Hanukiyah

Make a Hanukiyah from clay and/or wood. (Quick-drying clay is the easiest to use unless you have access to a kiln.) Either put a small block of wood in the middle or more clay to make the *shamash* higher than the other candles. Holes may be drilled in the wood if an adult is there to help. The holes should be just big enough to hold the candles. If you are using clay, make a hole with the candle and build up a collar round its base. Allow the clay to dry before removing the candle, but turn the candle once or twice to make sure it does not stick.

The Hanukiyah may be decorated with Hanukah symbols or the initial letters of the Hebrew words, which read 'A Great Miracle Happened There' (see below). Hebrew is read from right to left, rather than left to right as we read.

Dreidel

The *dreidel* is a game that is played at Hanukah. It is like a kind of top that spins. It is said that before the Maccabean revolt, when the Jews were not allowed to study their law, they would keep a top with them when they met together. If they were caught, they could truthfully claim that they were playing a game. The letters on the *dreidel* now remind them of the great miracle that happened in the Temple.

To make a very simple *dreidel* you will need some thin stiff card and a spent matchstick. Cut out a circle from the card and draw the letters as shown. Push the matchstick through the centre.

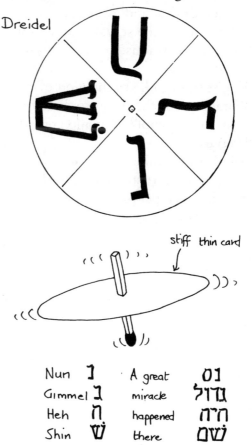

Dreidel

stiff thin card

Nun	נ	A great	ב	נ
Gimmel	ג	miracle	גדול	
Heh	ה	happened	הה	
Shin	ש	there	שם	

To play you will need lots of nuts, raisins or small sweets — divided equally amongst the players — and a bowl to go in the middle. Each person puts a nut (raisin or sweet) in the bowl. Each player spins the *dreidel* in turn. When the *dreidel* lands on the:

- *Nun* — nothing happens
- *Gimel* — that player takes everything from the bowl
- *Heh* — that player takes half the contents of the bowl
- *Shin* — that player has to put a nut into the bowl

All the players have to put a nut into the bowl after each turn. When players run out of nuts they are out. The winner is the player who ends up with all or most of the nuts.

PRAYER AND PRAISE

Light each of the candles of your Hanukiyah from the servant candle for each of these petitions:

1. I light this candle to the God of Abraham, for the promise that you gave to his people long ago and still keep today.
2. I light this candle to the God of Joseph, who trusted your word to save his own people and the Egyptians from famine.
3. I light this candle to the God of Moses, who led the Israelites out of Egypt and showed them your special rules.
4. I light this candle to the God of Joshua, who brought down the walls of Jericho with the sound of the trumpets.
5. I light this candle to the God of David, who put his trust in you enough to kill the giant, Goliath.
6. I light this candle to the God of Elijah, who trusted your power to light the altar that the prophets of Baal could not.
7. I light this candle to the God of Ezekiel, who trusted your love and hoped even in Exile.
8. I light this candle to the God of Judas Maccabeus, who saw the great miracle of the menorah in the Temple.

These candles are lit in the name of my God who loves me.

2 **Abba, Father, let me be**
42 **Father, I place into your hands**
242 **The Lord has need of me**
287 **Who is on the Lord's side?**
408 **Jesus put this song into our hearts**
447 **Praise and thanksgiving**

Eleven

ADVENT

INTRODUCTION

Advent is a time when we prepare for the celebration of one of the most important festivals in the Christian year. Almost everybody has heard about Christmas in this country. Even people who know nothing about Jesus celebrate with parties and giving presents at Christmas. However, to Christians, Christmas is much more important than just having parties and giving presents. It is the time when we remember how Jesus, the Son of God, was born on this earth to live as a human.

Such an important festival needs careful preparation if we are to make the best celebration.

STORY

The Annunciation
Luke 1:26–38
Excitement in Heaven (p. 128)

The time before Christmas is always very busy, but try to set aside a quiet time every day during Advent to think and read, in preparation for the festival.

ACTIVITIES

Advent wreath

Advent wreaths come in many shapes and sizes. They have four candles, one for each Sunday in Advent, with sometimes an extra Christmas candle in the middle. They are usually decorated

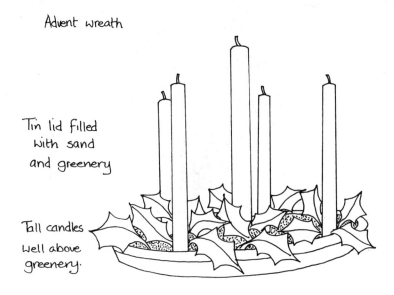

Advent wreath

Tin lid filled with sand and greenery

Tall candles well above greenery.

with evergreens. A deep tray of sand or two blocks of wet 'oasis', firmly held together, makes a good base for your Advent wreath. *Always make sure that greenery is not touching the candles as it can catch light.* One candle is lit on each Sunday through Advent so that on the Sunday before Christmas there should be four candles lit.

Advent tree calendar
You will need:
- *glue*
- *scissors*
- *large sheet of paper*
- *stiff green paper*
- *coloured paper*
- *old Christmas cards*
- *task instructions (see below) written on individual cards*

To make the calendar, cut out twenty-four diamond shapes from the stiff green paper. On the top half of each diamond stick on one of the task cards. On the reverse side of each diamond write a number from 1 to 24. Stick the diamonds to the sheet of paper in the form of a Christmas tree, gluing the *lower half only* to the paper. Every day in December fold down the top half of one diamond to reveal the day's task.

Make the shape of a tub with two doors from coloured paper. Stick the outside edges of the doors to a manger scene cut from an old Christmas card. Mount this under the tree and open the doors on Christmas Day.

If you like, you could stick a picture under the part of the diamond that will fold back. Cut small pictures from old cards. They will look like decorations on a tree.

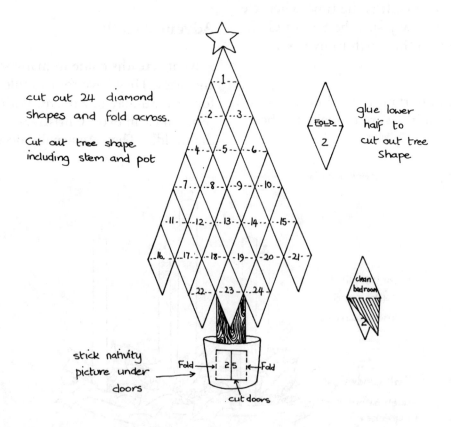

cut out 24 diamond
shapes and fold across.

Cut out tree shape
including stem and pot

glue lower
half to
cut out tree
shape

clean
bedroom

stick nativity
picture under
doors

Fold → 2|5 ←Fold

cut doors

Advent stockings calendar

You will need:

- *card*
- *scissors*
- *stapler or Blu-tack*
- *felt pens, crayons or wrapping paper*
- *string*
- *paper clips or small clothes pegs*
- *task instructions (see p.42) written on individual cards*

Cut out twenty-four pairs of different sized 'stockings' from card. Staple together each pair to make a container. Decorate with felt pens, crayons or wrapping paper as preferred. Write the numbers 1 to 24 on the stockings. Place each task instruction card inside the stocking with that number on it. If you didn't staple the stockings together, stick the instruction card to the back of the stocking with Blu-tack so that the edge of the instruction card appears to be coming out of the top. Hang the stockings on a piece of string with paper clips or tiny clothes pegs like socks on a clothes line. Each day in December remove that day's task card and carry out the instruction.

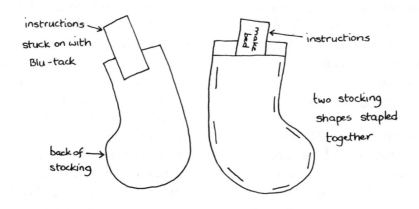

instructions stuck on with Blu-tack

back of stocking

instructions

two stocking shapes stapled together

Advent circle calendar

You will need:

- *2 large circles of card (one slightly larger than the other)*
- *old Christmas cards*
- *split-pin fastener*
- *scissors*
- *glue*
- *protractor*
- *compass; or string, drawing pin and pencil*
- *task instructions (see below) written on individual cards*

Make the circles as large as possible. Use a drawing pin, string and pencil if you don't have a large compass. Using the protractor, divide the larger circle into twenty-four sections — 15° for each section. Cut out one 15° section on the smaller piece of card, except for the part nearest the centre. Pin the circles together using the split-pin fastener.

Write the numbers 1 to 24 in the sections on the larger circle around the edge so that they show. Cut out the instruction and stick each one on to the appropriate section on the larger circle (they will be displayed as the smaller circle is turned round). Decorate the front of the smaller circle with old Christmas cards and the Advent prayer. You could cut out holly leaves and berries from green and red card and stick them on too.

Task instructions for the Advent calendars
On the four Sundays in Advent, in addition to the tasks below, light the candles on your Advent wreath.

1. Find a special way today in which you could help a relative or friend.
2. How could you help somebody who is not so fortunate as yourself? Perhaps you could find a good toy that you no longer use and take or send it to a charity shop. Ask first.
3. Sit quietly for a few minutes and think of all the refugees and poor people who (like Jesus) have nowhere to stay.
4. Draw as many different kinds of homes as you can think of.
5. Tomorrow is St Nicholas' Day. Could you send a little of your

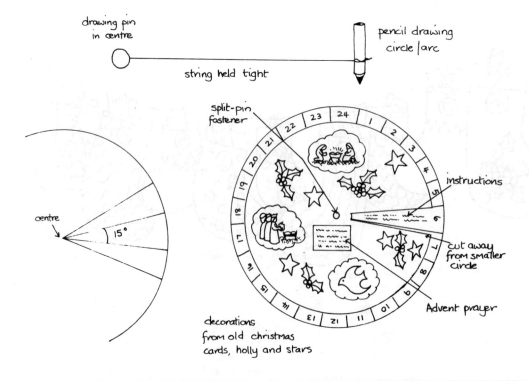

pocket money to a children's charity?

6. Find and read a story about St Nicholas.
7. Think what Christmas means to you.
8. Find a cardboard box. Paint it inside and out and stick some straw on the top and inside on the floor.
9. Make a donkey to carry Mary.
10. Make figures of Mary and Joseph.
11. Make some shepherds.
12. Make some animals for the stable.
13. Read how John the Baptist lived in the desert and baptized Jesus.
14. Draw a picture of John baptizing people by the river Jordan.
15. Find out when you were baptized. Who are your godparents?
16. Draw a picture of your baptism.
17. Make a baptism card for a baby welcoming him or her into the family of the Church.
18. Find the Welcome in the baptism service and write it out.
19. Read how the angel Gabriel came to Mary to tell her she would have a baby.
20. Draw a cartoon of yesterday's story. What did the angel say? What did Mary think? How did she tell Joseph? What did he think?
21. Sit quietly and think of how Mary must have felt as she waited for the birth of her baby.
22. Make a star and some angels to hang above your stable.
23. Make the baby Jesus in a crib.
24. Put the figures and animals in your stable.
25. Put Jesus in the stable and hang the star above it.

Advent prayer

Lord Jesus, thank you for coming to us at Christmas. As we prepare for this happy time, help us to remember what Christmas is all about. Remind us of how you want us to be. Help us to think of others and love them as you love us. Amen.

PRAYER AND PRAISE

The following may be used on each Sunday throughout Advent when the candles are lit on the Advent wreath.

Advent 1

Leader 1 The first Sunday in Advent reminds us that God's promise will soon come.

All   Watch and pray.

Leader 1 We must stay alert and ready, for the time of coming is nearer than expected.

All   Watch and pray.

Leader 2 I light this candle on the Advent wreath to remind us of the waiting time.

All   Watch and pray.

Leader 2 lights the first candle on the Advent wreath while a song is sung, e.g. 'Christmas is coming' from 'Innkeepers and Light Sleepers'.

Advent 2

Leader 1 The second Sunday in Advent remembers the prophets who told of the coming of a great leader, the Messiah, who would save the world.

All   Christ, the Saviour of the world.

Leader 1 The Bible tells the Word of God. Read, learn and act on God's holy Word.

All   Bless his holy Word.

Leader 2 I light this candle to remind us of the Word of the Lord.

All   **Bless his holy Word.**

Leader 2 lights the second candle on the Advent wreath.

Advent 3

Leader 1 The third Sunday in Advent reminds us of the message of John the Baptist who came to prepare the way for the coming of the Lord.

All   **Make a straight way for the Lord.**

Leader 1 Prepare yourselves for his coming.

All   **Come Lord Jesus!**

Leader 2 I light this candle on the Advent wreath to remind us of John the Baptist.

Leader 2 lights the third candle on the Advent wreath.

Advent 4

Leader 1 The fourth Sunday in Advent reminds us of the visit of the angel Gabriel to Mary.

All   **Blessed be the name of the Lord.**

Leader 1 'You will bear a son, and you shall call his name Jesus.'

All   **Blessed be the name of the Lord.**

Leader 2 I light this candle to remind us of the Virgin Mary, the Mother of the Lord.

Leader 2 lights the fourth candle on the Advent wreath.

Prayer
Loving God, may your gift to us of Jesus Christ set us free to love and serve others and to worship you with joy. Amen.

68 **Hark, the glad sound!**
186 **On Jordan's bank the Baptist's cry**
280 **When the Lord in glory comes**
362 **Hey! Hey! Anybody listening?**
427 **Make way, make way**
430 **Mighty in victory**
Carol Praise:
204 **Now tell us, gentle Mary**
286 **The angel Gabriel from heaven came**

Twelve

CHRISTINGLE

INTRODUCTION

It is only fairly recently that Christingle has been celebrated in Britain. It has come from the Moravian Church custom of giving lighted candles to children on Christmas Eve. The Children's Society liked the custom and adapted it to make it more appropriate for their needs. Services are usually held around the Christmas/Epiphany period.

The word Christingle means 'Christ Light'. The candle on the Christingle reminds us that Jesus is the 'Light of the world'; the orange on which the candle sits represents the world; the four sticks filled with sweets, nuts and raisins represent the four seasons and the 'fruits of the earth' — all the good things that God created for us. The red ribbon round the orange (world) reminds us of the blood shed by Jesus for us and the way in which Jesus died on a cruel cross.

ACTIVITIES

A Christingle
You will need:
- *an orange*
- *small candle*
- *silver foil or doily*
- *red ribbon*
- *four cocktail sticks*
- *sweets, nuts, raisins*
- *sticky tape*

Make a hole in the top of the orange and place over it the doily or a circle of silver foil. Push the candle well in to the hole. Thread the sweets, nuts and raisins on to the four cocktail sticks and push them into the orange around the candle. Wrap the ribbon around the middle of the orange and secure with tape.

Watch your own and other people's eyes on the sticks when carrying the Christingles and be careful with candles when they are lit. Keep the candle upright, but away from your face and hair and that of others near you.

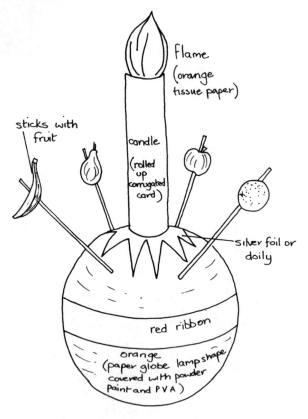

Flame (orange tissue paper)

sticks with fruit

candle (rolled up corrugated card)

silver foil or doily

red ribbon

orange (paper globe lampshape covered with powder paint and PVA)

small torch can be secured inside the 'flame')
- cocktail sticks — garden sticks or opened-up wire coat hangers
- sweets, etc. — larger pieces of fruit and vegetables

It will probably need to be kept upright by placing the whole thing in a shallow box, perhaps covered with silver foil and decorated with evergreens.

PRAYER AND PRAISE

The Children's Society produce some excellent material for Christingle services. Suitable hymns may include any that refer to Jesus as the 'Light of the world'.

Loving Father, help us to shine like the Christingle candle to remind others of your love for us all. Amen

  50 **Give me oil in my lamp**
128 **Jesus bids us shine**
315 **Bring your Christingle**
353 **God whose love is everywhere**
402 **It's rounded like an orange**
Mission Praise:
445 **Shine, Jesus, Shine (Lord the light of your love)**
420 **Like a candle flame**
643 **The earth was dark**

Display candle
A large display candle can be made by substituting the following for parts of the Christingle:

- orange — a paper globe lampshade covered with PVA glue mixed with orange powder paint
- candle — a large (Paschal) candle or rolled-up corrugated card with orange tissue paper for the flame (a

Thirteen

CHRISTMAS

INTRODUCTION

With all the excitement of Christmas — the parties, the presents, the food — we sometimes forget what Christmas is all about. This wonderful festival remembers when Jesus, the Son of God, came to the earth as a baby.

STORY

The Christmas story
Luke 2:4-20
Visitors in the night (p. 135)

ACTIVITIES

Figures for the stable
The following figures are very simple to make, even for very small children.
You will need:
- *card*
- *scissors*
- *felt pens or crayons*
- *scraps of material*
- *glue*
- *paper clips*
- *stapler*
- *cotton wool*

Cut out the semi-circle from card and wrap the ends round to make a shape like an upside-down ice-cream cone. Staple in place. This makes the body or

base of the figures. Cut out the arms and head. Push the head through the top of the base (you may need to snip off the top so that the neck can fit in). Curve the arms round a little. Find the centre of the arms and stick this to the centre of the back of the body. You may dress the cone figures with scrap material. If you prefer to colour the card with felt pens or crayons, it is wiser to do this *before* you wrap the base into a cone.

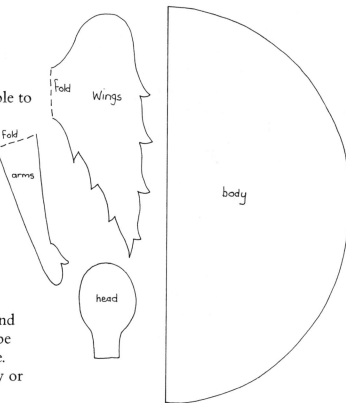

The animal figures simply need to be cut out of the card and folded as shown. Cut out ears, etc to stick on, and use felt pens to put in eyes and mouth, etc.

Cotton wool may be stuck to the body of the sheep. (To make a lying down sheep, simply cut off the legs!)

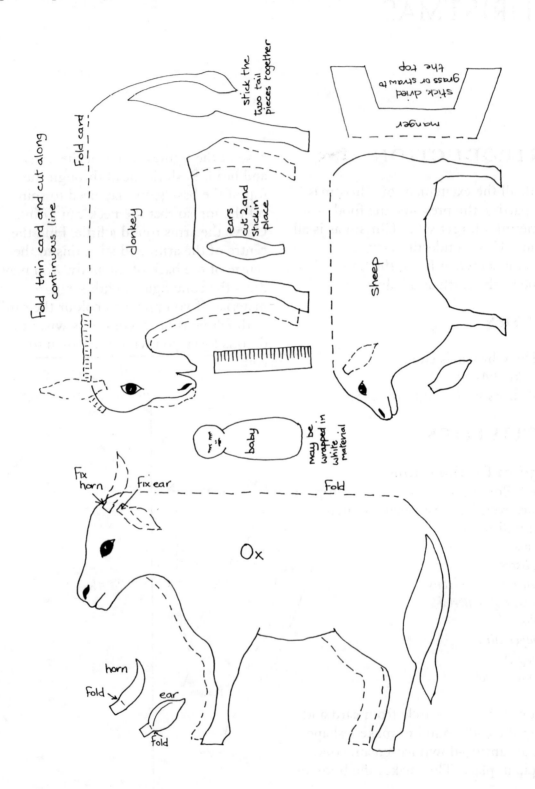

Decorated candles

Here are two very simple ways of decorating candles for use at Christmas. NOT FOR THE VERY YOUNG

1. You will need:
*   a thick candle
*   a lino-cutting tool (or similar)
*   fine paintbrush
*   gold paint mixed with a drop of washing-up liquid

Carefully chisel out star shapes all over the candle. Paint the stars using a fine paintbrush. Make sure that you do not get paint on the wick.

2. You will need:
*   a thick candle
*   coloured foil and sequins
*   a teaspoon which can be heated
*   scissors

Cut designs or patterns from foil, e.g. star shapes or silhouettes of stable a scene. Heat the teaspoon by standing it in very hot water for a while (make sure that the handle is not in the water). Position foil against the candle and press on with the spoon. Sequins may be pinned or stuck in place to give an extra sparkle, or as stars.

PRAYER AND PRAISE

Father in heaven, at this very busy time, if we forget you for a while, forgive us.

Jesus, son of Mary, at this very special time, if we do not always show others your love, forgive us.

Holy Spirit, at this very holy time, if we do not always behave very well, forgive us.

Help us to remember you at all times, to show your love to others and to behave in ways that will not make us or you ashamed. Amen.

Any Christmas hymns or carols. The following books may give you some new ideas:

Carol Praise
Innkeepers and Light Sleepers
Carol, gaily carol
Merrily to Bethlehem

Fourteen

NEW YEAR AND EPIPHANY

INTRODUCTION

New Year

The time just after Christmas may be rather dull and flat. During Christmas time there was probably so much excitement, with presents and parties; and most of us will have had too much to eat, and may have spent too much time watching the television and staying up late. It is sometimes quite hard to get back to the ordinary, everyday life we are used to.

It is at the New Year that many people make resolutions or promises. Sometimes the resolutions may be to stop eating so many sweets (because we ate too many at Christmas), or to go to bed early (because we stayed up late too often over Christmas and became grumpy). These may be very good resolutions but very often they are forgotten before long.

People in the Church may make resolutions too. In some churches, the first Sunday in the year is a very special day called Covenant Sunday. John Wesley introduced this idea nearly 250 years ago. 'Covenant' means promise and it is our promises to God that we remember at this time. We may have already made promises to God, or had promises made for us by godparents at our baptism. In the Old Testament of

the Bible we read how God made a covenant with Abraham: the people of Israel would be his people. In return, the people promised that they would obey God's laws. When Jesus came to the earth, he renewed that covenant — a covenant that had been broken by the people so often, but which God had kept all along. The Covenant service reminds us of those promises made long ago and of our own personal promises to God.

We do not know what God has in store for us. Not everything will be easy or comfortable, but God has promised that he will be with us. Can we keep to our side of the bargain? Can we obey God and put our lives completely in his hands? We know that keeping promises is not always easy, but God helps us if we really want to try. John Wesley knew how important it is to remind ourselves of promises made. Renewing those promises — saying them aloud together — helps us to keep them too. For your New Year resolutions you could try to remember those promises.

Epiphany

The first visitors to the stable in Bethlehem were the shepherds. They were the ordinary people from the village who would be well-known by everybody. The job of a shepherd was lonely and hard. He would often have to spend the night out with his sheep so he would not be the kind of person who was used to being with lots of people. In fact, many of the 'good citizens' of Bethlehem would not have spoken to shepherds! Nevertheless, God chose some shepherds to be the first to visit Jesus.

What would the shepherds have done when they returned from seeing Jesus in the stable? What would *you* have done if you had been there? Would you have told your family and friends? Perhaps the shepherds didn't have many friends or family, but if they did, what did the family and friends of the shepherds think?

It is likely that other villagers went to see Jesus and his mother Mary, although we do not hear about them in the Bible. Perhaps some of them became friends with the family and even helped Joseph to move the family into a little house.

Epiphany is the time when we remember the only other visitors that we know about from the gospel: the Wise Men. Remember that the gospel says nothing about kings, or how many Wise Men came, only that they came from the East and they brought gifts. Although they were welcomed in Bethlehem, they were unwelcome visitors to King Herod. When you have read the story, you may be able to tell why they were so unwelcome.

STORY

The visit of the Wise Men
Matthew 2:1-15
The evil plan (p. 136)

Most people who visit our homes are not so unusual. They do not usually bring such strange gifts, nor do their visits have such terrible consequences to the people of the town. Yet they have a very special influence on our lives. Think of all the people who come to your house. Some will be very welcome and invited in immediately. Others you may prefer not to see.

Think what happens when we know that visitors are coming? How do we prepare for their visit?

- tidy the house
- prepare a meal
- make the beds

What is really good about having visitors?

- extra special food
- some visitors are great fun to be with
- special outings and treats
- some bring lots of news

What is not so good about having visitors?

- having to be on our best behaviour
- having to move out of our bedroom
- endless 'grown-up' talk!

What about the unexpected visitors? Those that turn up on the doorstep?

What kind of host/hostess do you make? Do you make your guests feel welcome? Do you prepare yourself and your home for their visit?

What kind of visitor do you make? Are you polite and helpful? Would people want you to return?

Imagine that some very special visitors are coming to your house next week. Make a list of the things that you and your family will need to do.

Tell your best friend (or write a letter to a friend) how you feel about this visit. Think of all the excitement and pleasure you are feeling. Although there are a few things that are rather a nuisance, you really can't wait to see these visitors. Explain this to your friend.

Alternatively, pretend to be Mary or Joseph. How do you feel when the Wise Men come? What do you do when you see them coming? How do you make them welcome?

ACTIVITIES

New Year promises tree
Think of ways in which you can serve God better. Write or draw these on brightly coloured pieces of card. Attach them with thread to a bare branch stuck into a pot of damp sand.

Visitors mobile
You will need:
- *stiff card*
- *wire coat hangers*
- *thread and needle*

- *colouring pens or pencils*
- *scissors*

On stiff card draw a big picture of your home. Colour it and cut out the shape. Cut round the door and fold back so that it can open. Think of all the people that visit your home — e.g. the postman, the milkman, Granny and Grandad, your next-door neighbour. Draw as many of them as you can remember on stiff card. Draw the pictures in a simple shape like a circle or an egg shape so that they are easier to cut out. Attach to the wire coat hangers with thread so that they hang free.

PRAYER AND PRAISE

The prayer from session 19 (Shrove Tuesday, Ash Wednesday and Lent) could be used to recall promises.

Lord Jesus, you came to us as a baby. At this Epiphany time we remember when you were visited by the Wise Men. Help us to learn from those who visit our homes and those who visit our country. May we never be unready to welcome you into our homes. Amen.

Any of the usual carols that tell the story of the visit of the Wise Men would be suitable. (Remember that it is only tradition that has made the Wise Men into kings, and we do not know how many there were.)

  9 **As with gladness men of old**
251 **The Virgin Mary had a baby boy**
271 **We three kings**
Carol Praise:
 10 **A star in the sky**
 50 **Christ was born on Christmas Day**
146 **Jesus Christ the Lord is born**
155 **Kings came riding from the East**
278 **Soldiers marching**

Fifteen

CANDLEMAS

INTRODUCTION

The festival of Candlemas is celebrated on 2 February. It is sometimes called the Presentation of Christ in the Temple. Another name for this day is The Purification of the Blessed Virgin Mary.

There are very strict laws for newborn Jewish babies and their mothers. After the birth of a son the mother is thought to be 'unclean' and is therefore not allowed to touch anything holy. Thirty-three days after that she is at last considered to be 'clean' and so must show that she is fit to be with God again. She must give an offering, which could be a lamb and a pigeon or dove. If the woman is poor the lamb may be substituted for another pigeon or a dove. When she has made the offering, she is purified. You can read about these laws in Leviticus 12:1–8. Eight days after a boy is born he must go through a special ceremony called circumcision. The ceremony reminds them of their special relationship with God. A firstborn son is very special. He is believed to belong to God in a very special way. Parents must 'buy back' — 'redeem' is the proper word — their son. They would need five shekels. A shekel was a silver coin which was also used as a unit of weight (a little more than 10 grammes). See Numbers 18:15,16.

Candlemas remembers the time when Mary and Joseph took the month-old baby to the Temple to pay the 'redemption money' and to offer Jesus to God in his service. Here they met two old people, ordinary but good people, who lived in Jerusalem. When they saw Jesus, these people immediately knew how very important he was or would be.

Due to its connection with Jesus, the Light of the world, Candlemas is being used increasingly as the time to hold a Christingle service, especially as it fills a rather quiet time in the Church's year.

STORY

The presentation of Jesus in the Temple
Luke 2:21–40

ACTIVITY

'Light' stained glass windows
Even the smallest child can help with this activity.
You will need:
- *two pieces of clear sticky-back plastic each, the size of your design*
- *lots of different colours of tissue paper*
- *a permanent black felt pen*

Design your own picture on the theme of 'light' on ordinary paper. Make the

Use a permanent black felt pen to go round the design. This will cover any ragged edges on the tissue paper. Hang up your stained glass window against a window. The light will shine through just like a real window.

Some may like to symbolize light, rather than just use a candle. Some may show Jesus as the Light of the world and others may make a picture of Jesus as a baby with Mary, Joseph, Anna and Simeon in the Temple.

PRAYER AND PRAISE

Procession of candles

Have small candles prepared by pushing them through circles of card with a small hole in the centre. This protects hands and other surfaces from dripping wax. Each participant will need a candle. Make the building as dark as possible. Stand in silence.

Leader   Jesus, you are my light:

All   Shine your light on me.

A big candle may be lit on the altar or central table.

Leader   Jesus Christ is the Light of the world:

All   Shine your light on me.

Candles around the central candle are lit from that candle and passed on to light all the candles whilst a hymn/song is sung.*

Prayer
Jesus, you are the Light of the world. You give light to guide us in our darkness. As we light our candles we

design bold and clear; don't put in too much detail. Place half the sticky–back plastic on top of your design. Pull back the protective cover so that the sticky side of the plastic is on top. You should be able to see your design through the plastic.

Tear the tissue paper into small pieces (not more than about 5 cm. across, not less than 1 cm.) and place them on the sticky plastic to correspond with your design. When the design is covered, stick the second piece of plastic on top of the design. This is quite tricky, so be very patient. It may be a good idea to get somebody to help you with this. This should have made a 'sandwich' with the tissue paper pattern as the filling.

* Mission Praise 445 Shine, Jesus, Shine (Lord the light of your love). Alternatively the lighting of the candles may be done in silence with only the words: **Jesus is the Light of the world** *as each person lights another candle. This may be followed by the singing of the hymn/song.*

see the building fill with light and warmth. In the same way, as we tell others of your Good News, the whole world may be filled with your love, reflected by those who love you and try to follow you. Amen.

The words of the Nunc Dimittis *(the Song of Simeon) may be read or sung here.*

Carol Praise:
179 **Lord, now let your servant depart in peace**

180 Lord, now let your servant go his way in peace

The candles may be carried in procession whilst an easy, simple and repetitive hymn/song is sung (i.e. one for which there is no need for words to be carried e.g. 'Give me oil in my lamp').

  50 **Give me oil in my lamp**
128 **Jesus bids us shine**
424 **Lord, you are the Light**
456 **Sing and celebrate**

Sixteen

JESUS THE TEACHER AND HEALER

INTRODUCTION

Jesus lived as a human to show us how people should live. We know little about his early life, but he probably learned the trade of Joseph, the carpenter. We know that he had several brothers and sisters so he was probably kept busy helping Mary and Joseph to look after them.

When he was about thirty, Jesus left home and began the special work for which he had come. He spent only about three years travelling around with his disciples, teaching the people and healing the sick. Although this time was short, there are so many remarkable things to learn about his life and work. He did many wonderful things.

STORY

The Lord's Prayer
Matthew 6:9-13

ACTIVITIES

The Lord's Prayer
Jesus taught us to pray. In Jerusalem, there is a church where the Lord's Prayer is written in many different languages. Write out the Lord's Prayer and illustrate it with pictures of ways in which we can do what the prayer says. Think carefully about what the prayer suggests. We say the prayer so often that we sometimes forget what we are really saying.

Zig-Zag pictures
You will need:
• *a long, narrow sheet of paper or card*
• *felt pens or crayons*

Fold the paper/card so that it makes a zig-zag book. Draw events and teaching in the life of Jesus on each fold of the zig-zag. You could include:

• healing of Jairus' daughter
• story of the Sower
• the Good Samaritan
• the Lord's Prayer
• the Sermon on the Mount
• the feeding of the 5,000
• the story of the lost son (the Prodigal Son)
• choosing the twelve disciples
• and any more of your favourite stories and events.

Blockbuster quiz
The game may be played like the television game or simply by putting each of the questions on a separate piece of card with the initial letter, printed large, on the other side. For the Blockbuster game you will need to cut out lots of hexagons (six sided shapes), printing the initial letter on one side and the corresponding question on the

other. Shuffle the cards so that they do not come out in alphabetical order.

A One of Jesus' disciples who brought his brother to follow Jesus. John 1:40-42

B The place where Mary and Martha lived. John 11:1-2

C A town on the lake where the Roman centurion lived who asked Jesus to heal his servant. Luke 7:1-10

D Jesus rode into Jerusalem on the back of one of these. Matthew 21:1-5

E The country to which Jesus and his family escaped from Herod. Matthew 2:13-15

F The number of people fed by Jesus on the mountain side. Matthew 14:13-21

G The name of an area and large lake in northern Israel where Jesus and many of his disciples came from. Luke 4:14

H The king who had John the Baptist beheaded. Matthew 14:1-12

I The Good Samaritan took the injured man to this place. Luke 10:34

J His daughter died but Jesus made her well again. Mark 5:22

K A valley between Jerusalem and the Mount of Olives. John 18:1

L Brother of Mary and Martha. John 11:1-2

M One of the twelve disciples who was a tax collector. Matthew 9:9

N A Pharisee who asked Jesus questions. John 3:1

O The Mount of _ _ _ _ _ _. Luke 19:29-38

P Friend of Jesus, whose name means 'the Rock'. John 1:42

R The Jews had to pay taxes to Caesar who was the Emperor of this place. Luke 20:20-26

S Jesus had one or two arguments with these and the Pharisees. Matthew 16:1

T The place where Jesus was found when Mary and Joseph thought he was lost. Luke 2:41-52

V Jesus said that he was like this (a plant on which grapes grow). John 15:1

W Where Jesus went and was tempted. Matthew 4:1-11

Y A wooden collar to hold oxen together. Luke 14:19

Z This little tax collector climbed a tree to see Jesus. Luke 19:1-10

Answers are at the end of the book.

PRAYER AND PRAISE

Say or sing the Lord's Prayer.

 23 **By blue Galilee**
192 **Our Father who is in Heaven (Caribbean Lord's Prayer)**
197 **Peter and James and John**
286 **Who took fish and bread**
387 **If you love me**
397 **It was Jesus who taught his disciples**
451 **See the man walking**

Seventeen

THE GOOD SAMARITAN

INTRODUCTION

Jesus told some of the greatest stories ever. One of the most well-known is the story of the Good Samaritan. The Jews had many enemies and the people of Samaria were amongst them. Long before, the people of Israel had been exiled to what is now part of Iran. In exchange, people from that area came to live in the fertile land of Israel. When the Jews returned, they hated the people who had turned them out of their homes. Jesus gave a strange message to those Jews in this story — that they should love and care for everybody, even those who were considered to have wronged them. We must listen to that message too if we are to do the will of God.

STORY

The Good Samaritan
Luke 10:25-37
Danger on the lonely road (p. 166)

ACTIVITIES

Good Samaritan moving picture
You will need:
- *five pieces of card (see illustrations)*
- *scissors*
- *felt pens or crayons*
- *sticky tape*

On the biggest piece of card, draw a scene of the road from Jerusalem to Jericho. You will need two large rocks and plenty of smaller ones. Draw the injured man, unconscious on the ground, in the centre, foreground of your picture. On the two big rocks, cut and fold back 'doors'. Between these cut out completely a shape that will be big enough to reveal figures of the people in the story.

On the longer, narrower piece of card draw the three characters in the story that travel on the road — the priest, the Levite and the Good Samaritan himself. You may like to draw the road in the background. On the two small pieces of card draw robbers. They need to be stuck securely behind the doors in the rocks.

Lastly, tape another piece of card onto the back of the biggest piece. The long, narrow piece should be able to slide comfortably between the two, revealing the three travellers in the gap. Tell the story to your friends whilst moving the doors and characters on your picture.

Zig-zag pictures
Make a zig-zag book as in session 16. On each fold draw part of the story of the Good Samaritan. Make sure to get the story in the right order. (It may help to draw the story on separate pieces of paper and then stick them to the folds.)

cut and fold back doors in rocks

cut out and remove

stick pictures of robbers inside double doors in rocks

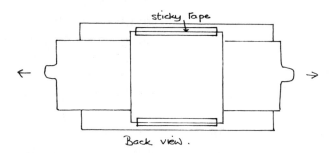

sticky tape

Back view.

hold sliding picture in place with piece of thin card taped to back of main picture.

PRAYER AND PRAISE

Thank you, Jesus, for all the wonderful stories that you told. Help us to understand the full meaning of those stories and to live our lives as you wish us to. Help us to care for others as the Good Samaritan cared for the stranger. Amen.

95 **If you see someone lying in the road**
228 **Tell me the stories of Jesus**
405 **Jerusalem man**
443 **Once upon a time**

Eighteen

JESUS, FRIEND OF SINNERS

INTRODUCTION

The Gospel Story — the story of the life and work of Jesus — gives us a very special message: God really loves us, even when we do wrong. Jesus once told a wonderful story about a young man who did some very foolish, selfish things but his father still loved him and welcomed him back. This story is often called 'The Prodigal Son'. 'Prodigal' means wasteful — somebody who spends without thinking.

STORY

The Prodigal Son
Luke 15:11–32
The Boy who ran away (p. 164)

Imagine that you are the brother of the Prodigal Son — the other son. You have worked hard on the farm all your life while your younger brother went off and wasted his inheritance on parties and other things. How do you feel about your brother and the way that your father has welcomed him back?

Have you ever felt that way? — cross because you have been good and not had any special reward, whilst somebody else was naughty and rewarded when they were sorry? Have you ever thought, 'It's not fair!'? Most people will have felt that way at some time, but is it how God wants us to be?

God is sad when we behave badly, but he is happy to forgive us when we are sorry and try to do better — just like the father was with the Prodigal Son. None of us is good *all* the time. We are glad to be forgiven when we have done wrong. God has lots of love to go round. Just because he forgives us when we have done wrong, it doesn't mean that he loves us any less when we are good.

When we are cross — jealous and envious — we become rather like an apple with a grub inside. On the outside, the apple looks perfect — rosy and good to eat — but as soon as we bite into the apple we realize that it is not so good. The grub has eaten away the tasty flesh and left a brown mess. When we are jealous we become like the apple — fine on the outside, but inside we are eaten up with jealousy and unable to see the bad in ourselves. God wants us to be like the perfect apple but he loves us even with the grub inside. Every time you eat an apple try to remember God's love for all of us — all the time — good or bad.

ACTIVITIES

Good Apple, Bad Apple
Cut out two apple shapes, exactly the same. Colour one a nice rosy red. On

the other, draw the core and a grub eating its way through the good flesh inside. Pin the two apples together with the rosy one on top. Think of how you can be the rosy apple. How can you stop the grub from growing inside you?

Prodigal Son tableaux

A 'tableau' is a picture made up from people — rather like a still photograph, or when you pause a video in the middle of the action. A story is told with a series of these pictures, these tableaux.

You will need these characters:

- Prodigal Son
- Father
- Other Son
- 'friends' of the Prodigal Son
- pigs
- neighbours of the family

Decide which scenes will make the best tableaux or use the following:

- the Prodigal looks fed up — he wants more excitement in his life
- the Father divides the money between the sons
- the Prodigal sets off on his journey
- the Other Son works hard on the farm
- the Prodigal spends all his money enjoying himself with his (so-called) friends
- the 'friends' desert him when there is no money left
- the Prodigal is left to look after the pigs
- the Prodigal returns to his Father
- the Father is very glad to see him and welcomes him with open arms
- the Prodigal asks his Father to forgive him and to take him back as a servant
- the Father calls for the best feast to be laid on

- friends and neighbours come to celebrate the return of the lost son
- the Other Son will not join in because he is so cross

Box TV

You will need:

Box television
- *a large, strong cardboard box*
- *pencil and ruler*
- *craft knife or sharp scissors (adult help needed)*
- *broom handle cut in half*
- *coloured sticky-back plastic, wallpaper or paint*
- *four fruit juice bottle tops*

Story scroll
- *roll of wallpaper*
- *sheets of paper*
- *sticky tape or glue*
- *crayons, felt pens or paints*
- *stapler*

Cut off the flaps from the top of the box. This will be the back of your TV. Make sure that the bottom of the box is securely taped. This will become the front of your TV. Rule a rectangle or square on the front of the box like the screen of a television. *Very carefully* cut out the shape with the knife or scissors.

The broom handles are needed to hold the pictures in a kind of scroll. As they are turned, the story is shown through the hole or 'screen'. You will need to make holes for the broom handles to slot in on the top and bottom sides of the box, on either side of the screen. The holes should be just big enough for the handles to slide through. Cover the outside of the box with wallpaper or sticky-back plastic or paint. Add a little PVA glue to the paint so that it will cover even the tape. It may help to fix 'feet' on the bottom of your TV. Bottle tops from fruit juice bottles stuck on the bottom will hold the box level.

Decide which pictures will tell the story. (You could use the suggestions for the tableaux above.) Make sure that each piece of paper is just slightly smaller than the whole front of the box. Draw or paint these pictures. Remember that the top and bottom of the paper will be hidden behind the edges of the front of the TV screen. On one sheet you could put the title (or name of the story) and even the names of those of you who drew the pictures.

Arrange the pictures in the order they come in the story. Stick them on to the wallpaper firmly with sticky tape or glue. Put the broom handles in place so that the ends stick out at the top and bottom of the box. Attach one end of the roll to one of the handles: this may need glue and tape. Staples would make it even more secure but that needs great care. Make sure that the pictures are facing the front and show through the 'screen'. Wind most of the roll around that handle. Attach the other end of the roll to the other handle.

As the story is told, one of the handles should be turned. If you are very clever, make the box so that you can replace the scroll with other stories and use it again and again. The top or the bottom of your TV will have to be moveable.

PRAYER AND PRAISE

Leader   Heavenly Father, you know our faults better than we do, we bring before you all that we have done wrong today/this week.

All   **Forgive us our trespasses.**

(Silence while we think about those things we have done wrong.)

Leader   Jesus, friend of sinners and saints,

All   **Help us to be sorry when we have sinned, and modest when we are saints.**

(Silence while we consider what it means to be forgiven.)

Leader   Holy Spirit, we want to do better.

All   **Lead us in the way of goodness.**

(Silence while we think of ways in which we may do better.)

Lord, you are the friend of everybody, even those who have done wrong. I am sorry for all that I have done wrong. As you forgive me, help me to forgive myself and those who I have wronged. I make this pledge to you to try to do better in the future. Help me not to judge what others do but to concentrate on my own behaviour. Help me to be the kind of person with whom lonely people may find friendship, and sad people may find a smile to make them cheerful. Help me to show to others the kind of love and care that you show to me. Amen.

27   **Cleanse me from my sin, Lord**
43   **Father, lead me day by day**
371 **I look out through the doorway**
460 **Sometimes I'm naughty**
463 **Sorry Lord**

Nineteen

SHROVE TUESDAY, ASH WEDNESDAY AND LENT

INTRODUCTION

If we had celebrations every day of the year they would all become ordinary. We need quieter times in between so that we can really appreciate and enjoy the special occasions. There is one festival in the Church year that stands out as being the most wonderful of them all: Easter. Just as we prepare for Christmas with the season of Advent, we have a quiet time of preparation for Easter with the season of Lent.

SHROVE TUESDAY

There are not so many people now who remember Lent as strictly as in the past, but there are still many who make special preparations during this time. Many people make it a time of 'self-denial': that means that they do not allow themselves special treats of any kind. They eat little, and what they do eat is plain and simple food. They do not have parties or drink alcohol. On the day before Ash Wednesday — Shrove Tuesday — all the rich foods are eaten up and many people have a 'last fling' party before the serious time of Lent.

In some countries they hold a great carnival, which is like a huge party in the streets — the last party allowed before Easter. The word 'carnival' is probably made up from the two Latin words that mean 'meat' and 'goodbye' — Goodbye to meat! In other places Shrove Tuesday is called *Mardi Gras*, which means 'fat Tuesday' — the day when all the fats and other rich foods are eaten up.

What is another name for Shrove Tuesday? (*Pancake Tuesday*) Why is it called that? (*All those foods forbidden in Lent may be eaten up in pancakes.*)

Many people 'give up' something for Lent. We may give up sweets or try not to swear or use bad language, or perhaps try to stop shouting at each other. We may try and *do* something that will help to make us better people. It is not always easy to keep to the promises we make to ourselves, but we try. To be able to start afresh, we need to say how sorry we are for what we have done wrong, ask forgiveness for those wrong things and promise to try to do better in the future. After we have done this before God we are considered to be 'free from sin' or to use the old word — 'shriven'. On 'Shrove' Tuesday we are 'shriven'.

ACTIVITY

Pancakes
Most people have their own favourite

recipe for pancakes. The following is a very simple version:

200g flour
4 eggs (this can be reduced)
1 pint milk
a pinch of salt

Mix these all together well until they form a 'runny' consistency. Use an old cup to pour the mixture onto a little hot fat melted in a frying pan. Spread the mixture by tilting the pan backwards and forwards. When the top has dried, turn the pancake with a fish slice or, if you are very clever, toss it with a flick of the wrist. *Do this very carefully.* Cook until both sides are the colour of toast.

To serve, cover with sugar and lemon juice and roll like a carpet. Other fillings may include raisins, honey, jam, syrup, etc.

ASH WEDNESDAY

Ash Wednesday marks the beginning of the solemn time of Lent. After all the parties of Shrove Tuesday, people would be 'shriven' — made free from sin — to be able to carry out the solemn tasks of Lent. On Ash Wednesday the palm crosses from the year before were burned. The ash from these would be used to make the sign of the cross on the 'shriven' person's forehead, visible to everybody. This old practice is continued in some churches today.

The custom of using ash dates from biblical times. When people wanted to show that they had turned from all the wrong things that they had done and promised to try to do better, they would sprinkle themselves with ashes and wear a rough garment of sackcloth. This would itch and scratch and remind them constantly of their promises.

PRAYER AND PRAISE

To recall the Ash Wednesday practice yourself you will need:
- *palm crosses from last year (If these are not available, paper crosses made in the same way may be used.)*
- *a metal bowl in which to burn the crosses (adult help required)*

As the crosses burn, the following prayers could be used:

Leader Father in Heaven, please remember us as we begin this solemn time of Lent. We are sorry for all the times when we have let you down.

All Lord, we are sorry. Please forgive us.

Leader For the times when we listened to the voice in our heads even when we knew it was wrong:

All Lord, we are sorry. Please forgive us.

Leader For the people we have hurt in thought or deed.

All Lord, we are sorry. Help them to forgive us.

Leader	For the things we did not do that could have helped others.
All	**Lord, we are sorry. Help us forgive ourselves.**
Leader	For the opportunity to start afresh.
All	**Thank you Lord.**
Leader	For the opportunity to do better.
All	**Thank you Lord.**
Leader	We make this promise before you and before everybody here that we will try to do your will more each day.
All	**We promise.**
Leader	Forgive us our sins as we forgive those who sin against us.
All	**Lord, help us to know your forgiveness.**
Leader	Father be with us and guard us through the coming days.
All	**Grant us your peace.**
Leader	Let the sign of the cross remind us of your love for us and help us to be more like you.
All	**Lord bless us and keep us.**

Each person may dip a finger in the ash and mark him/herself or a neighbour with the sign of the cross. In most churches the marking of the cross with the ash and the absolution (or the words spoken to tell us of God's forgiveness) are traditionally spoken by a priest.

LENT

Lent begins on Ash Wednesday and lasts for forty days and nights. This recalls the time that Jesus went into the desert to think things out and to talk with God without interruptions. He spent forty days and nights in the desert without proper food or drink.

STORY

The temptation of Jesus in the wilderness
Matthew 4:1-11; Luke 4:1-13
The Battle with Satan (p. 142)

Different translations use different names for the 'voice inside our heads' that tries to get us to do things that we know are wrong. Some translations refer to Satan, others to the devil.

ACTIVITIES

Choices game
The Choices game from session 4 could be used here to remind us of the temptations that Jesus faced and the choices that he had to make.

Temptation sketches

In groups of three or four make up a story about temptation — an incident when somebody was tempted to do something they knew to be wrong. Using your own words or just mime, act the story for the others. It should be clear *what* the temptation is. Does the person give in to temptation? Decide what happens:

- if he/she gives way to temptation
- if he/she resists temptation

You could use some of the stories from the Choices game to set you off.

Lent calendar

Draw or paint a picture of Jesus in the wilderness. Place self-adhesive circles (like stones) on the picture, one for each day of Lent. You will need forty of them. Write numbers 1 to 40 on the circles. The list opposite indicates a possible reading for each day. Alternatively, you could take a reading from one of the many published Bible reading notes.

PRAYER AND PRAISE

See Ash Wednesday prayers above.

- 27 **Cleanse me from my sin, Lord**
- 41 **Father, hear the prayer we offer**
- 43 **Father, lead me day by day**
- 152 **Let us praise God together**
- 212 **Search me, O God**
- 307 **All you have to do**
- 460 **Sometimes I'm naughty**
- 463 **Sorry Lord**

Mission Praise:
- 160 **Forty days and forty nights**

Day	Bible Reading	
1.	Genesis 12:1-20	The call of Abraham
2.	Genesis 15:1-21	God's promise to Abraham
3.	Genesis 21:1-8	Isaac is born
4.	Genesis 22:1-19	Abraham is tested
5.	Genesis 37:1-3	Jacob's family
6.	Genesis 37:4-11	Joseph's dreams
7.	Genesis 37:12-24	The brothers' revenge.
8.	Genesis 37:25-36	Joseph is taken to Egypt
9.	Genesis 39:1-23	Joseph in prison
10.	Genesis 40:1-23	Joseph interprets dreams
11.	Genesis 41:1-36	Pharaoh's dreams
12.	Genesis 41:37-57	Governor of Egypt
13.	Genesis 42:1-38	Jacob's family needs food
14.	Genesis 44:1-34	The missing cup
15.	Genesis 45-46:27	The brothers are sorry
16.	Exodus 2:1-10	Moses in the bulrushes
17.	Exodus 2:11-25	Moses has to leave Egypt
18.	Exodus 3:1-22	The Burning Bush
19.	Exodus 5:1-21	Moses and Pharaoh
20.	Exodus 7:14-10:29	The Plagues
21.	Exodus 12:1-36	The Passover
22.	Exodus 13:17-14:31	Crossing the Red Sea
23.	Exodus 16:1-36	Food in the desert
24.	Exodus 17:1-7	Water in the desert
25.	Exodus 19:1-25	Mount Sinai
26.	Exodus 20:1-17	The Ten Commandments
27.	Exodus 25, 26 and 27	God's special tent
28.	Exodus 31:18-32:35	A golden calf
29.	Exodus 34:10-35	God's promise to Moses
30.	Joshua 2:1-24	Spies in Jericho
31.	Joshua 6:1-25	Joshua and the walls of Jericho
32.	1 Samuel 7:15-10:16	A king for Israel
33.	1 Samuel 16:1-17:54	David
34.	1 Kings 1:11-3:28	Solomon the wise king
35.	1 Kings 6:1-38	Temple in Jerusalem
36.	1 Kings 12:1-24	Israel is divided
37.	1 Kings 18:20-40	God versus Baal
38.	1 Kings 19:1-18	The still, small voice
39.	2 Kings 2:1-16	Elisha
40.	2 Kings 5:1-27	Naaman is cured

Twenty

FRIENDS

INTRODUCTION

What is a friend? Some of us have lots of friends and we spend a lot of time with them. We may play together, make things together, go to school together. Some of us have only one or two friends. We prefer to spend more time by ourselves and only need to meet up with friends for short times. Some of us are very shy and find it difficult to talk with others. We may have very few or no friends. Sometimes we even find imaginary friends. They are not real people but we can talk to them and play with them as if they are real. Your best friends may be brothers or sisters.

What makes a good friend? Is it somebody who

- is fun to be with?
- shares our interests?
- is a good listener?

Are your friends good friends? If they asked themselves the same questions about you, what would their answers be? Would you be found to be a good friend?

The following is a story about four friends who were very good friends. They would not give up until they had found help for the man who was unable to walk.

STORY

The four friends
Luke 5:17–26
The hole in the roof (p. 154)

ACTIVITIES

Peter's house

You will need:
- *card*
- *crayons or felt pens*
- *scissors*
- *split-pin fastener*

Cut a large circle from card. As shown on the illustration, draw pictures on the circle (in clockwise order):

a. friends with the paralytic man
b. friends looking through hole in the roof
c. Jesus teaching people in the house
d. Jesus with the healed man

Cut card to make the house. There should be steps up the side and a door in the middle. The door will need to be quite big so that your pictures will be seen. Cut and fold the door back. Place the circle behind the house and secure with a split-pin fastener. Tell the story as you turn the circle to reveal the scenes.

If this is too difficult, make two houses

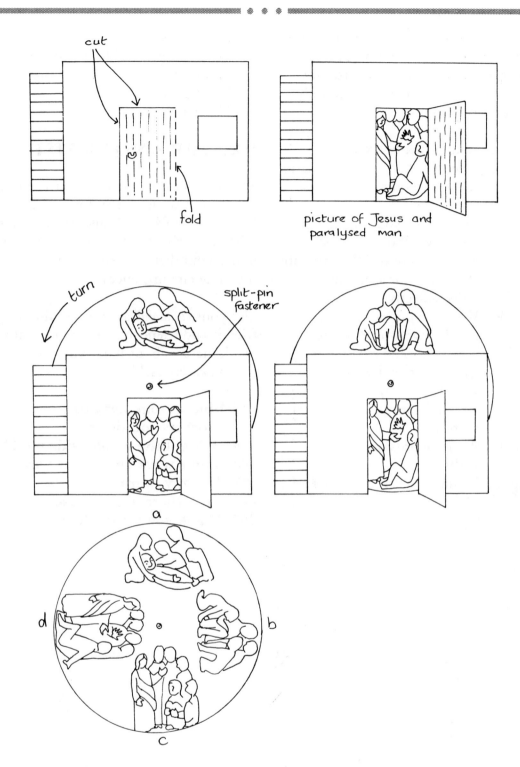

exactly the same from card. On separate sheets of paper, draw the pictures to go behind the door and on the roof. Stick the houses side by side on a piece of background paper with the pictures behind so that they show the two scenes — before and after the friends have let down the sick man to Jesus.

A poem about friends

A *cinquaine* is a good way of making up a poem. It is a five-line poem. Make up your own *cinquaine* or work in a small group.

It may help to have pieces of card cut from five different colours (one colour for each line of the poem). Each person writes his/her suggestion on the appropriate colour and the cards are pooled. You may decide to keep only the best suggestions.

The following is just one way of making a *cinquaine*, but it doesn't matter how you make up yours.

Line 1: The title of your poem, e.g. 'My Friend' or 'Friends'
Line 2: Words or phrases that describe the title — these are often called adjectives.
Line 3: Words or phrases that answer how? why? when? where? what? etc. These words often end in '-ly' and are called adverbs. If they are difficult, just find some more describing words.
Line 4: Action words or phrases — verbs
Line 5: Nouns (naming words) that say more about the first line.

My friend
Funny, happy, with lots of ideas.
Always there when I need him.
Playing football together,
My mate!

PRAYER AND PRAISE

Think about how we treat our friends. Sometimes we let them down as Peter let down his friend, Jesus. Are we angry when our friends let *us* down, or do we understand that we may do the same in the same circumstances?

Use your *cinquaine* as a prayer about friends and friendship. Think carefully and honestly about what kind of friend you make yourself.

17 **Bind us together Lord**
21 **Brothers and sisters**
78 **He's got the whole wide world**
108 **In our work and in our play**
302 **A naggy mum**
444 **Once there was a house**
467 **Thank you for the love**

Twenty-one

PASSOVER

INTRODUCTION

The Feast of Passover is now usually considered just a Jewish festival. We sometimes forget that Jesus himself was a Jew. He would have been taught the Law and stories from the Torah (the first five books of what we call the Old Testament). With his family and friends, he would celebrate the feasts and festivals of the Jewish year. In the gospels that tell about the life of Jesus, we read more than once that the Passover was one Jewish feast that Jesus celebrated. Jesus went with his parents to celebrate Passover in Jerusalem when they lost him and found him in the Temple (Luke 2:41-52). Later Jesus celebrated the Passover in the Upper Room with his disciples, even though he knew it was dangerous for him to enter Jerusalem (Matthew 26:1—30).

Passover remembers the time when the Israelites who had been slaves in Egypt were at last able to escape, with God's help of course.

STORY

Escape from Egypt
Exodus 8 to 12
Too many frogs (p. 36)
Blood on the door (p. 39)

ACTIVITIES

Passover frieze

The Passover itself refers to the last and most terrible plague, when the Angel of Death 'passed over' the homes of the Israelites. However, to get the whole picture, we need to know the rest of the story — the other nine plagues.

Illustrate the story with a long frieze. Use lots of different fabrics and papers, cut out and stuck onto background paper. This could be a plain roll of wallpaper. You could show all the plagues along an Egyptian scene. In the middle put Pharaoh, looking very fierce and saying 'No!' to Moses who asks if Pharaoh will let his people go.

The plagues are these:

1. All the waters of Egypt turn to blood
2. Frogs
3. Maggots (some translations say gnats)
4. Swarms of flies
5. Disease killing cows and other animals belonging to the Egyptians
6. Painful boils
7. Hailstones
8. Locusts eating all the crops
9. Darkness
10. The firstborn son of every Egyptian family dies

Remember that the Israelites are safe from all these plagues. At the end there would be the Israelites, dressed ready for their journey, standing to eat the meal of roast lamb. Blood will be smeared on the doorposts so that the Angel of Death knows which houses to pass over.

Plague circle
You will need:
- *two circles of card*
- *ruler and protractor*
- *felt pens or crayons*
- *scissors*
- *split-pin fastener*

Divide one circle into ten sections with the ruler and protractor. In each of the sections, draw the plagues in the order that they happened. On the other circle cut out just one section but *do not go right up to the centre*. Place this circle on top of the other so that the cut out part reveals one of the plagues. Secure the two circles together at the centre with the split-pin fastener.

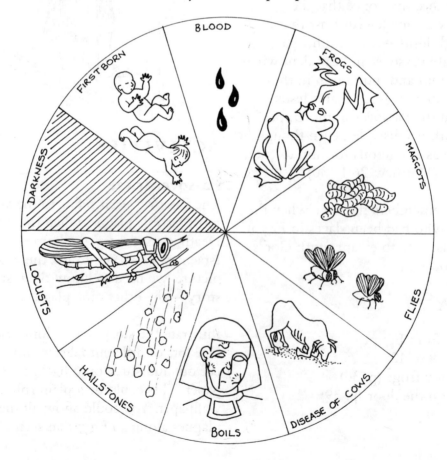

Decorate the top circle with scenes of Egypt (the pyramids, palm trees, slaves making bricks, the Egyptian Pharaoh, or simply geometrical designs). As the circle is turned it should reveal the ten plagues.

Passover meal

The Passover itself refers to the way the Angel of the Lord, who brought death to the Egyptians, 'passed over' the homes of the Israelites. God's people had been told to smear the doorpost of their homes with the blood of a lamb. The firstborn sons of the Egyptians died (even the son of Pharaoh), but all the Israelites were safe. They ate a meal of roast lamb with bread that had no yeast and bitter herbs. This they ate standing up and dressed for a journey. They needed to be ready to go as soon as Pharaoh let them.

This meal, or something to remind them of it, is eaten in Jewish households at Passover. The youngest member of the family asks why they are holding this feast and the father or head of the family tells the story of the escape from Egypt. There are lots of books that help to explain more about how Jews celebrate the Passover feast. You could have your own Passover feast.

Remember to tell the story of how God helped the people of Israel to escape from their slavery in Egypt.

Passover music

The Roger Jones musical *From Pharaoh to Freedom* tells the story of that escape, and how Jesus later used part of the ceremony in the Last Supper to remind us of him. This musical has some songs that tell the story and help to bring it to life. You may like to listen to (and sing) some of the songs and even act out the story. Particularly useful may be the song about the plagues — 'Let's Go, Pharaoh!' — and the Passover of the Angel of Death — 'When I see the Blood I will pass over you'. In 'Let's Go Pharaoh!' there is plenty of chance to act the plagues, and you could even make up your own Egyptian dance.

PRAYER AND PRAISE

From Pharaoh to Freedom
by Roger Jones

2 Abba, Father, let me be
22 Be still and know that I am God
81 Hévénu shalom aléchem
82 How great is our God!
276 When Israel was in Egypt's land

Twenty-two

MOTHERING SUNDAY

INTRODUCTION

During the long, serious time of Lent there is need for a little break from all the fasting and 'self-denial' — a short time when we can relax the strict rules. This time is supplied by Mothering Sunday, the fourth Sunday in Lent. Another name given to the day is Refreshment Sunday.

At first, this had nothing to do with mothers. It was Mother Church that was the focus for attention. Like many other Christian festivals, Mothering Sunday has its origins in ancient times, before the love of God in Jesus was known in these islands. The Romans worshipped a goddess who represented motherhood. In spring, the earth was like a mother giving birth to all the new things of life — plants and animals, birds and insects. The Christian Church took this over as a festival to remember Mother Church. A good mother loves and cares for her children. Mother Church loves and cares for her family.

As this was the only 'time off' — holiday — in the long period of Lent, it became the time when people would go 'home to Mother' to visit her. They would often take a gift — perhaps flowers collected on the long walk home. The festival gradually became a celebration of all mothers.

STORY

Although the two ladies in the story had many problems, they loved and cared for each other as mother and daughter.

Ruth and Naomi
Book of Ruth
The foreigner (p. 56)

ACTIVITIES

Not everyone lives with a mother but you could make any of these gifts for whoever cares for you — mother, father, granny, aunty etc.

Mothering Sunday basket
You will need:
- *A4 stiff paper or card*
- *scissors*
- *crayons or other form of decoration*
- *glue or staples*

Fold the paper/card in half. Fold the outer edges in to the centre fold. Open this out and repeat the process from the other end (see diagram). This should leave sixteen smaller rectangles in the folds. Run your thumb nail along each fold to make a very firm fold.

From one short end, cut off four of these small rectangles. *Do not discard!* If you are using crayons, decorate the card

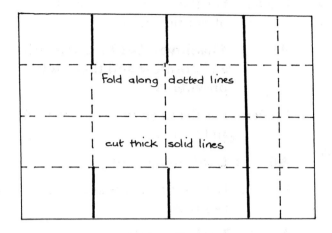

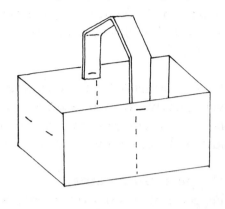

with flowers, patterns, etc. On the twelve rectangles make four small cuts as shown on the diagram. Fold up to make a box. Stick firmly or staple the ends in place. Fold the remaining four rectangles lengthways in half. Stick firmly or staple the ends in position as the handle for the basket.

If you wish to decorate the basket with e.g. tissue paper flowers this can be done now. The basket may be filled with biscuits, sweets (e.g. Peppermint creams) or even flowers. Crunch up tissue paper or a paper serviette lightly to make a base for the gift, or place a doily at the bottom of the basket.

Pop-up Mothering Sunday Card

You will need:
- card and scrap card
- scissors
- felt pens
- glue

Fold one sheet of card in half. Cut a small square from the scrap card. Fold this in half. Fold the ends back the other way. Line up against the inside edge of the larger card so that it makes a 'step' when it is held open. Glue the edges of the 'step' to the inside of the card. Secure this with paper clips while the glue dries.

Use the felt pens to make a design on the front of the card. Repeat this on another sheet of card. Cut this out and

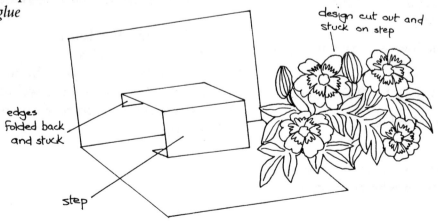

stick it on the front of the step when it stands up. (Make sure that it is not too big as it should be hidden when the card is closed.)

Do not forget to write your greeting very clearly. You will want to show how much you love your mother/carer just as she or he loves and cares for you.

Peppermint creams
Peppermint creams do not need cooking facilities. You will need:
- *sifted icing sugar*
- *peppermint essence*
- *milk*
- *vegetable colouring*
- *a bowl and mixing spoon*
- *greaseproof paper*
- *tea cloth*

Mix the ingredients to a stiff paste. Roll small lumps of the paste into balls. Flatten the balls and lay them to dry on greaseproof paper. When dry on one side, turn over to dry on the underside. Dust with icing sugar. They will require covering lightly with a tea cloth during this process.

PRAYER AND PRAISE

Leader: Families are people who share their lives. We give thanks for families.

All: Thank you Lord for families.

Leader: For the love we share amongst us.

All: Thank you Lord for love.

Leader: For the food we share together.

All: Thank you Lord for the food and those who prepare it.

Leader: For the warmth and comfort of our homes.

All: Thank you Lord for warmth and comfort and those who provide it.

Leader: For the times when we quarrel and fight . . .

All: Lord, we are sorry.

Leader: For the times we have refused to share . . .

All: Lord, we are sorry.

Leader: For the times we have hurt one another . . .

All: Lord, we are sorry.

Leader: For our selfishness in only wanting the best for ourselves . . .

All: Forgive us Lord, and help us to do better.

Leader: For the lonely and sad . . .

All: Be with them and help us to share with them.

Leader: For the tired and the ill . . .

All: Bless them and comfort them.

Leader: For the whole family of the Church.

All: Help us to be a loving, caring, happy family. Amen

17 Bind us together Lord
21 Brothers and sisters
42 Father, I place into your hands
78 He's got the whole wide world
301 Lord we ask now to receive your blessing

Twenty-three

HOLY WEEK AND EASTER

INTRODUCTION

Although these may be separate stories in their own right, some of the activities are linked here because the story is needed as a whole. The Crucifixion should not be seen as the end, but the end of the beginning! Also, many churches have Holy Week holiday clubs and the activities suggested here are particularly useful for that kind of occasion, and especially for an all-age event.

STORIES

Entry into Jerusalem and the cleansing of the Temple
Matthew 21:1-17
The day Jesus cried (p. 178)
The day Jesus was angry (p. 146)

The Last Supper and the Garden of Gethsemane
Mark 14:12-51
The traitor (p. 180)
Soldiers in the night (p. 182)

Trial and crucifixion
Matthew 27; Mark 15; Luke 23; John 18:12 — 19:42
The day the sun could not shine (p. 184)

Easter morning
Matthew 28; Mark 16; Luke 24; John 20
The empty grave (p. 186)

As with the Christmas story, the gospel writers tell different parts of the story. Like all of us, they remembered different things about the time.

JERUSALEM JOURNEY

Participants are divided into three groups and each of the groups explore part of the story through drama, music, or art and craft. For the next part of the story, each group moves on and explores through another activity. In that way each group will have covered the whole story but will have explored it in different ways. At the end of the day, what has been learned can be presented in the form of worship. All the participants could move from place to place to tell the story. e.g. you could start outside to tell the Palm Sunday story, and even go upstairs (if that is possible) to an 'Upper Room' for the Last Supper.

Drama
You will need:
- *the Bible story (as many versions as possible)*
- *simple costumes (tunics, dressing gowns and tea towels as used in Nativity plays)*
- *large sheets of paper*
- *felt pens*

Read the story carefully more than once. You may need to leave out some parts of the story, so decide which parts are the most important to tell and which parts may be left out without spoiling it. Decide how best you can tell the story to others. For example, it may be best for one person to read the story while the others mime. Or you could read from one of the dramatised versions of the Bible, where several people say the words of different characters in the story. You may prefer to tell the story in your own words. Try to imagine how those people would have felt.

You may like the 'audience' to join in by becoming part of the crowd (coming into Jerusalem, at the trial, before Pilate and at the crucifixion). You could write the words that they should shout on the sheets of paper. Make the writing as big and clear as possible.

Music

There are many songs and hymns that tell different parts of the story (see 'Prayer and Music' section). Do not try to learn too many new songs at one time. There are plenty of well-known hymns/songs. Look carefully at the words. They will tell the story but will also show how the people who were there felt, and perhaps how we feel too. If you cannot find appropriate songs you could make up your own, or you could play instrumental music that reflects the way people felt at the time.

Art and Craft

You will need:

- *seven large cardboard boxes (square if possible)*
- *scrap material*
- *scissors*
- *PVA (or similar) glue*
- *a broom handle, pole or stick*

When placed on top of each other, the boxes will make a very big cross. The 'arms' of the cross will have to be held up with the pole. This can go right through the centre of the three boxes on that level. If the boxes are not all the same size, place the bigger ones at the bottom.

Each of the boxes will tell one part of the story — starting at the bottom:

- the entry into Jerusalem
- in the Temple
- the Last Supper
- the Garden of Gethsemane
- the trial
- the crucifixion
- Easter morning

Make up a picture of that part of the story on each box with collage materials or, if you prefer, by painting, or a mixture of both. You can go all the way round most of the boxes, but remember that they will be placed on top of each other, so the top and bottom of the boxes will not be seen. It may be best to put the crucifixion box right in the middle. There will only be two faces showing on that box, and those on either side will probably only need three faces illustrated (although the bottom of these may be seen so will need to be tidy).

The top box will be the Easter story, when Jesus is alive again. This is such an important and wonderful part of the story that it could be different. It could be made by cutting out the sides of the box and replacing them with 'stained glass windows' showing the scene (see session 15). A light could be placed inside this box to make the pictures shine like a real window. (Always ask an adult to help with this.)

If you are using the cross as part of the presentation of the story with the drama and the music, each box could be collected at the appropriate part of the story and built up to make the cross.

HOLY WEEK TREASURE TRAIL

The Treasure Trail map tells the whole Holy Week and Easter story.

Participants could be in small groups of all ages and abilities. They can physically move round the room to different locations where the questions and 'treasure' objects are. When a question is answered each group may collect the 'treasure' that represents that part of the story. However, 'treasure' is not collected at every point. On their personal maps they can draw and stick on a small badge for each part of the story. They then move on to the next part of the story.

There are ten points on this trail but it could be added to, or some could be left out. Groups could perform the suggested tasks too (optional). Questions and activities may be adjusted to suit the age/ability. It may help to have a really big copy of the map for the whole group.

At each point on the Treasure Trail:

- read the story
- answer the question
- collect your treasure
- make your badge to stick on your map

Trail Point	Bible Reading	Badge/ Picture	Treasure
1. Entry into Jerusalem	Mark 11:1—10	palm tree	palm cross
2. Cleansing the Temple	Mark 11:15—17	coin	coin
3. The Last Supper	Mark 14:22—26	chalice (cup)	bread/wine
4. Agony in the Garden	Mark 14:32—42	praying hands	stone/prayer
5. Arrest and trial	Mark 14:43—65	handcuffs	
6. Peter's Denial	Mark 14:66—72	cock	feather
7. Pilate's soldiers	Mark 15:15—20	crown of thorns	thorns
8. Crucifixion	Mark 15:22—37	cross	nail
9. Burial	Mark 15:42—47	perfume	dab of perfume
10. Jesus is alive	Mark 16:1—11	empty tomb	Easter Egg

Think of your own design for the pictures and suggest other treasures: you do not have to stick to those suggested. These further 'treasure points' could be added:

- Judas the Traitor   Matthew 26:14-16; 27:3-10   bag of coins
- Barabbas   Luke 23:13-25
- Simon of Cyrene   Luke 23:26

Suggested questions for the Treasure Trail

You may well think of better questions.

1. Jesus' entry into Jerusalem
What were the two towns called near the Mount of Olives?
What did the people shout?
Task: Make a palm cross from a strip of paper.

2. Cleansing the Temple
Into what did Jesus say the people had turned the Temple?
Task: Make a scroll. Write on it: My Temple shall be a house where people from all nations will pray.

3. The Last Supper
What did Jesus give his disciples to eat and drink?
Task: Draw a picture of the twelve disciples with Jesus at the Last Supper.

4. Jesus in the Garden of Gethsemane
Who were the three friends who went with Jesus to the Garden?
Task: Write a prayer asking God's forgiveness for all the wrong things we do.

5. Arrest and trial
What did the people at the trial do to Jesus?
Task: If you were arrested for being a Christian would there be enough evidence to convict you? Think about this question and how you could change to be more like Jesus.

6. Peter's Denial
How many times did Peter say that he did not know Jesus?
Task: Sing the song 'Peter's Denial' from *Jerusalem Joy.*

7. Pilate's Soldiers
Where did the soldier's take Jesus after the trial?
Task: Make a crown of thorns.

8. Crucifixion
What does 'Golgotha' mean?
Task: Use percussion and other musical instruments to show the sadness of that Good Friday.

9. Burial
Who was the man who went to Pilate to ask for the body of Jesus?
Task: Make a garden with the tomb on a tray.

10. Jesus is alive
Who was the first person to see that Jesus was alive?
Task: Write a newspaper article telling the 'Good News'.

Key to the map

1. Gate into Jerusalem/Jesus' entry into Jerusalem
2. Temple/ceansing the Temple

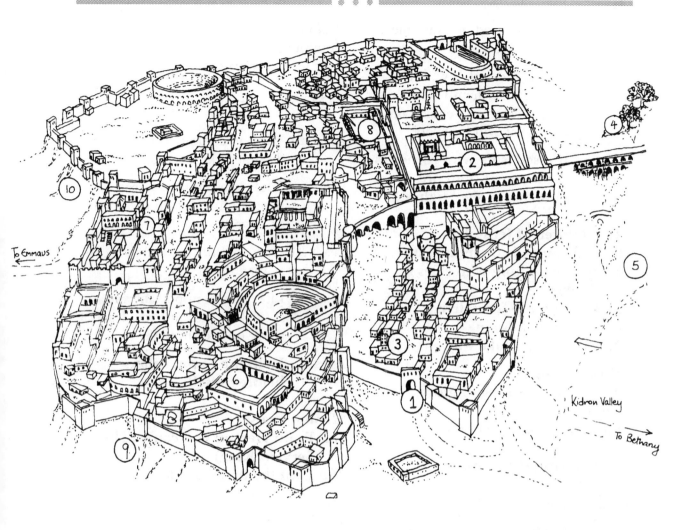

3. Upper Room/Last Supper
4. Garden of Gethsemane
5. Mount of Olives
6. High Priest's house
7. Herod's palace
8. Roman fortress of Antonia
9. Golgotha (Calvary)
10. Jesus' tomb

PRAYER AND MUSIC

Each 'station' of the Holy Week story Treasure Trail or the Jerusalem Journey could incorporate the following prayer and music suggestions. The leaders may be adult or children. Leader 1 stands back to explain what is happening. Standing back allows a clearer picture of events. The other leaders are in the story, witnessing and involved. They are tossed by the tide of events, confused and frightened and react to events accordingly much as the first disciples and onlookers must have done. The words of Jesus and Peter are included at times. How will we respond to the pain we see and the actions Jesus asks us to take?

Some songs tell the whole story so you could use a verse for each part. Also, the traditional Stations of the Cross can be used in place of these.

1. Palm Sunday — entry into Jerusalem

Leader 1 Lord, you come to the city,
riding on an ordinary donkey,
not a proud horse. You are

King and God, yet humble as the poorest man.

Leader 2 I stand and watch with the crowd. Like them I shout your praise. What excitement and joy! What will Jesus do?

All **Blessed is he who comes in the name of the Lord. Hosanna in the Highest!**

24 **Children of Jerusalem**
209 **Ride on, ride on in majesty**
264 **We have a king who rides a donkey**
354 **Going up to Jerusalem**
365 **Hosanna, hosanna**
427 **Make way, make way**

Mission Praise:
790 **You are the king of glory**
Jerusalem Joy:
Jesus rode a donkey into town

2. Cleansing the Temple

Leader 1 Lord, you are angry . . .

Jesus   My house shall be a house of prayer, but you have made it a den of thieves.

Leader 2 What have you done, Jesus? You have made dangerous enemies!

Leader 1 You stand for good and right — not the good and right of man, but of God.

Leader 2 I stand back. I do not want to be involved.

All **Help me to see all that is wrong and evil in the world. Help me to stand up for what is good and right.**

Jerusalem Joy:
In the Temple

Wild Goose Songs Vol 2 (Iona Community):
Jesus Christ is waiting

3. The Last Supper

Leader 1 Lord, you come to your disciples like a servant.

Peter   You wash my feet! Great people must not do the work of slaves!

Leader 1 God does not measure success as man does.

Leader 2 I like to feel important and special. You shame me, Jesus; I think only of myself.

All **Help me to put others before myself.**

Mission Praise
162 **From Heaven you came (The Servant King)**
261 **I am the bread of life**

Jerusalem Joy:
The Last Supper

4. The Garden of Gethsemane

Leader 1 Lord, you know what is in store for you. You are afraid, yet you will not turn back.

Jesus   Not what I want but what you want, Father.

Leader 2 I don't understand — we won't let him die!

Jesus   Couldn't you watch with me just one hour? Watch and pray.

Leader 3 I am tired, so tired. I will help . . . tomorrow.

All **The spirit is willing but the flesh is weak. Watch and pray.**

341 From Heaven you came (The Servant King)

Jerusalem Joy:
Gethsemane
Wild Goose Songs Vol 2:
Watch, watch and pray

5. Arrest and trial

Leader 1 A friend has betrayed you, Lord. He did not understand what you had to do.

Leader 2 You brought it on yourself, Jesus! Why don't you call down an army of angels to save you?

Leader 1 Your friends desert you. You are taken like a criminal.

Leader 2 There are too many of them. We can't fight alone.

All   When we are lonely and afraid God stands with us.

Jerusalem Joy:
The Trial

6. Peter's denial

Leader 1 You were with Jesus.

Peter: I have never seen him before.

Leader 2 You know Jesus.

Peter   I do not know that man.

Leader 3 You *must* know him.

Peter   I tell you, I do not know Jesus.

Leader 4 A cock crowed.

Silence

Jesus   Before the cock crows, you will say three times that you do not know me.

All   Lord I know and love you.

May I never be afraid to tell of your love.

Jerusalem Joy:
Peter's denial
English Praise:
Bitter was the night

7. Pilate's soldiers

Leader 1 The soldiers beat you and mock you.

Leader 2 He is weak. He doesn't even try to fight back.

Leader 1 They place a crown of thorns on your head. They spit on you and hit you.

Leader 2 Long live the King of the Jews (*jeering*).

All   When I forget you, I put more thorns on your head. Hold me close.

304 A purple robe

8. Crucifixion

Leader 1 You hang on the cross, broken and dying.

Leader 2 Why did I run away? Lord, I love you. You did this for me.

Jesus   My God, my God, why have you forsaken me?

Leader 3 Surely he was the Son of God.

Silence

91 I danced in the morning (Lord of the Dance)
245 There is a green hill
269 Were you there when they crucified my Lord?
304 A purple robe

Jerusalem Joy:
The Crucifixion

9. Burial

Leader 1 They take you down from the cross.

Leader 2 I cannot hide the tears

Leader 1 They bury your body in a cave. The stone is rolled across the entrance.

Leader 2 Jesus, I wish I had done more for you when you were alive.

All   **Jesus, you gave yourself for me — to die on a cross.**

Silence

65 Go, tell it on the mountain

Mission Praise:
346 **It is a thing most wonderful**
755 **When I survey the wondrous cross**

Jerusalem Joy:
It is over now

10. Jesus is alive

Leader 1 The night is over. The sun has come up. Jesus is alive!

All   **Alleluia! Christ is risen!**

Leader 2 I see your face but I can hardly believe it.

All   **Alleluia! Christ is risen!**

Leader 2 It is you. Alleluia! Christ is risen!

Leader 1 Jesus is alive!

All   **Alleluia! Jesus is alive!**

151 **Led like a lamb**
256 **This joyful Eastertide**
299 **Yours be the glory**
320 **Children join the celebration**
449 **Roll the stone**
457 **Sing and celebrate**
469 **The Lord is risen today**

472 The Spirit lives (Walk in the light)

Jerusalem Song:
He's not here for he is risen

ALTERNATIVE ACTIVITIES

I was there!
You will need:
• *a Bible*
• *an encyclopaedia of the Bible or similar (optional)*

Use what evidence is available, along with your own imagination, to begin to understand some of what the people involved in the Holy Week and Easter stories must have felt. Tell a partner, or write a letter telling what you saw and how you felt. You may like to write a poem or song instead.

These are some of the people that were there. Each of them has a very different part of the story to tell.

• John — at the Last Supper
• Peter — when he denied that he even knew Jesus
• Judas — who betrayed Jesus to the soldiers and helped them arrest him
• Pilate — who tried Jesus and, although he knew that Jesus was innocent, ordered his crucifixion
• Barabbas — a guerilla fighter, who had killed and fought but was let off instead of Jesus
• Caiaphas — the High Priest who brought Jesus to Pilate
• Simon of Cyrene — who carried Jesus' cross
• Mary, Jesus' Mother — who wept at the foot of the cross as she saw him die

Easter newspaper

Tell the wonderful events on Easter Day in the form of a newspaper. This could include interviews with various characters who witnessed the events, e.g. Peter, a guard, Pilate, Caiaphas. Of course you will need pictures (photographs) of these people. There may be a recipe for the Passover, a quiz or crossword, an editorial, sports news, fashion report etc.

Palm cross

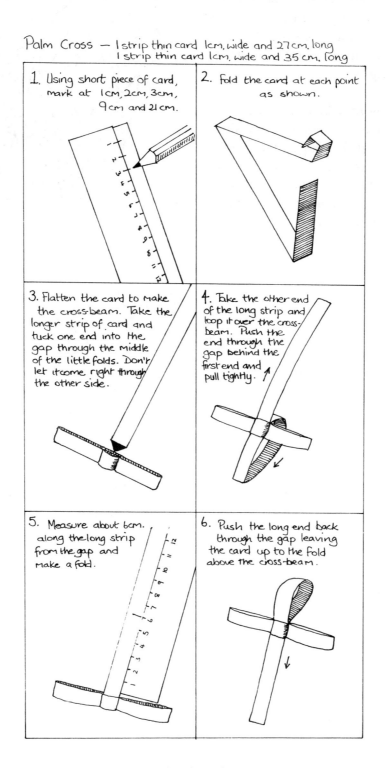

Palm Cross — 1 strip thin card 1cm. wide and 27cm. long
1 strip thin card 1cm. wide and 35 cm. long

1. Using short piece of card, mark at 1cm, 2cm, 3cm, 9cm and 21cm.

2. Fold the card at each point as shown.

3. Flatten the card to make the cross-beam. Take the longer strip of card and tuck one end into the gap through the middle of the little folds. Don't let it come right through the other side.

4. Take the other end of the long strip and loop it over the cross-beam. Push the end through the gap behind the first end and pull tightly.

5. Measure about 6cm. along the long strip from the gap and make a fold.

6. Push the long end back through the gap leaving the card up to the fold above the cross-beam.

Good Friday/Easter Egg

Cut out a large Easter Egg shape from card. Cut across the egg as if it had cracked open. On this egg draw or write some of the things that represent the bad things in the world. On separate pieces of card draw or write the good things in the world today. Attach then as if they are bursting out of the cracked egg. Jesus brought all the good things when he burst out of the tomb on that Easter morning.

The same thing may be done with a Good Friday/Easter cross. On one side are pictures of all that is good and on the reverse are pictures of all that is bad. This can be hung up so that both sides can be seen or put on a box cross like the Jerusalem Journey cross.

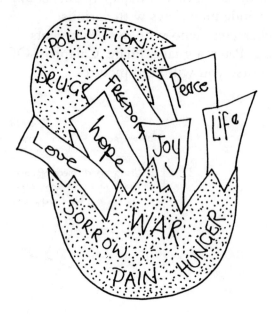

Twenty-four

CHRISTIAN MISSION AND AID AGENCIES

INTRODUCTION

Most people will have seen dreadful pictures of starving people — mainly in Africa. Although we see the pictures quite frequently, it is difficult for us, who are well fed, to imagine or understand what it is like to be really hungry. If we miss a meal or two or are even late for a meal, for whatever reason, we begin to feel hungry — tummies 'rumble' and may even feel a little uncomfortable. So many people in Africa (and other parts of the world) will not just feel uncomfortable. The hunger never goes away because there is never enough for them to eat. They begin to feel very tired and weak — unable to do much — like when you have a bad bout of flu. We get better from flu but without food and medical aid those starving people will never be healthy. Many will die.

What makes this even worse is that it should never happen. There are droughts (when no rain falls for long periods) which make it difficult for crops to grow, but in the world there is *enough for everybody*. God has given the world plenty for all our needs. However, people all over the world have been and *are* greedy. We take far more than we need of the world's resources and waste what we don't use.

There are many ways in which we in the Western world, in particular, waste our resources. We have mountains of food stocked for years. We cut down forests to make mountains of paper. We fail to re-cycle materials that *could* be used again. As well as all this, wars are being fought which stop vital food supplies reaching starving people.

We are not *better* than these starving and oppressed people, just *luckier*. God loves us all equally. Most of us in the Western world, just because we happen to live there, have more than enough.

Many people remember those who are not so well off as themselves and they are working to try and change all this. In May of each year an envelope is pushed through the letterbox of most houses in this country. The envelope will have written on it: Christian Aid Week. Christian Aid is just one of the many Christian agencies that work to help people all over the world. The people who work for Christian Aid do it because that is what they believe God wants them to do.

STORY

How Christian Aid began
In 1944, near the end of the Second World War, thousands of people in Europe were without food and homes.

British people had been through a dreadful war but most of them had not been so badly affected as those in the rest of Europe. Christians in Britain decided that they must help all these refugees. They raised about a million pounds. (That is a lot of money even today but in those days, when times were very hard, it was an amazing amount.) The money was used to feed the hungry in Europe, rehouse those whose homes had been destroyed, repair damaged churches and help Christian ministers to do their vital work amongst desperate people, and to 'pick up the pieces' of the broken world.

Gradually, as Europe recovered, it was realized that there was still a desperate need in other continents. The British Council of Churches (or Inter-Church Aid as it was called then) sent help for refugees and victims of all sorts of disasters and wars. However, they slowly began to see that it was not just when there was a disaster or war that there were people in need. In 1957 Inter-Church Aid decided to have a special week of events and door-to-door collections. It was called 'Christian Aid Week'. This was so successful that they decided to make it a regular, annual event. In 1964 Inter-Church Aid changed its name to Christian Aid.

Christian Aid does not just remember other Christians. It tries to work to help all those in need, whatever their religion, colour, or in fact wherever they live. Jesus said: 'Whenever you help others, however poor, you have been helping me.' Christian Aid, like all the other Christian agencies, tries to do what Jesus taught.

Christian Aid is supported by Christians from many different churches but it is only one of many agencies. Can you think of other agencies that constantly work to help others in the world? There are some that are not just Christian. Don't think that it is just Christians that give generously to help others. For example, Muslims and Jews give a tenth of all they have to help the poor. How many Christians could claim to give anywhere near as much as that?

God has given us so much. We only have to look at the trees, flowers, animals and birds. We only have to look at our full plates. God has provided us with all that we need to eat. Even so, there are millions in the world who go hungry. How can that be?

STORY

The parable of the sheep and the goats
Matthew 25:31-46

This Bible reading is remembered in the story of *Papa Panov* (also sometimes known as *Martin the Cobbler*) by Leo Tolstoy. It is available in book form or even on video. The story is often used at Christmas but it can be told at any time.

ACTIVITIES

Aid for Those in Need

We may think there are few ways in which we can help others. Fortunately it is unlikely that we will come across a man who has been mugged on the roadside, as for instance the Good Samaritan did. However, there are many ways in which we can help those that suffer, in whatever form. It does not need to be anything grand. Jesus said that even the smallest kindness would count.

You can support the work of whatever Christian agency you prefer by:

"please help me "

fill her food bowl —

give generously.

- finding out more about their work
- telling other people about their work
- giving money
- finding ways of earning money to give to the agency
- praying for their work

My Food for the Day

You will need:

- *plain paper plates*
- *scrap material/felt pens/crayons*
- *pictures from magazines*
- *empty packets of foodstuffs*
- *scissors and glue*

Think what you ate for breakfast, lunch, tea and supper (or whatever you call your meals). You may have had snacks in between. Draw or paint on the plates; or cut out from magazines, scrap

Breakfast
Weetabix and tea

Lunch
Sausage, beans, chips, orange juice

Tea
Cheese and tomato sandwich, tea

Supper
Apple, packet of crisps

material or packets, and stick them onto the plates, all that you eat on a normal day.

Compare this with what a child in East Africa might eat (if he had anything) — perhaps a little rice and very little water. This will have to feed him for the whole day. You almost certainly have plenty to eat and drink, with lots of choice.

In the Western world we eat more food than we really need. We throw away and waste enough to feed thousands of starving people. God gave us this food. Does he intend millions to die because they have not enough to eat? What can we do to help?

The unequal shopping game

Collect a few 'check-out' till receipts. Compile a shopping list for a family, using the receipts as reminders. Collect some of the items on your list — empty packets will do. Price the goods. Make sure that you have a bag of rice amongst those things. Arrange the goods to look

as much like a shop as possible. Put the rice with a small glass of water in a separate place.

You will need some 'toy' money. This can be made if there is no *Monopoly*-type money available. Divide your group into two unequal groups. Give the larger group a very small amount of the money: not quite enough to buy the bag of rice. Give the other group the rest of the money. Allow the small group the first choice of the shopping. When nearly all the goods have been taken, send in the large group to purchase the rice.

At this stage, the 'game' is over. What will you do? How can you remedy this extremely unfair situation? Have you even noticed that it is unfair?

Collage

Collect pictures from the newspapers of some of the events that cause such dreadful suffering to so many, e.g. drought, war, disease, famine, earthquake, etc. You may be able to find pictures too of people helping those who are in trouble. Make a collage of them all so that you may concentrate on them in your prayers.

Cinquaine

You may like to write a *cinquaine* (instructions are in session 20). This could be used for your prayers. The following are a few examples:

Refugees
Hungry and homeless
Families and friends dead or dying
Hold out a bowl for food
Will you feed them?

Pain
Sick, dying
Exhausted and desperate

Lie there, waiting to die
Does nobody care?

PRAYER AND PRAISE

Make up your own prayers or use the following:

Leader: Heavenly Father, you have made enough for everybody.

All: Thank you for your great gifts to us.

Leader: You are sad when you see those who are starving and hurt.

All: Help us to see them too.

Leader: You want us to care about these people and to share with them the plenty that we have.

All: Help us to care.

Leader: Bless those who suffer from lack of food; comfort those who have lost their families and homes because of war; heal those who are sick.

All: Help us to do those things in your name

Leader: Teach the leaders of the nations ways of peace; help all people to share when they have so much; bless those who try their best to help others in trouble.

All: Teach us your ways, Lord.

  5 **All over the world**
 47 **For I'm building a people of power**
 95 **If you see someone lying in the road**
123 **I will make you fishers of men**
124 **I want to walk with Jesus Christ**
161 **Make me a channel of your peace**
275 **When I needed a neighbour**
380 **I'm going to stand up**
416 **Let's go and tell our friends**
498 **Would you walk by (Cross over the road)**

Twenty-five

ASCENSION

INTRODUCTION

The followers of Jesus, his disciples, were ordinary people (like the first visitors at his birth). Jesus had twelve special disciples that he chose to be with him in his work. Some were fishermen. Can you name any of the disciples who were fishermen? Can you name the tax collector amongst the twelve disciples?*

After the death of Jesus, his disciples were frightened and of course very sad. Three days later, Jesus was alive. We call this wonderful happening the Resurrection. It is difficult to imagine how the disciples must have felt. They would have been overjoyed to have Jesus back with them, but they must have been confused and perhaps still rather fearful.

It must have been wonderful having Jesus back with them after that dreadful fright when he died on a cross. But things were different. Jesus did not travel around talking to the people he met. It was only his followers who saw Jesus. He was definitely alive; he wasn't a ghost. They could touch him and he ate with them, but it felt as if he was

*Answers: Peter and his brother Andrew, James and his brother John were fishermen. Matthew was a tax collector. (Zaccheus *was* a tax collector, but he was *not* one of the twelve.)

preparing them for when he would not be there.

STORY

The Ascension
Acts 1:1-11

ACTIVITIES

Footprints
This little story is very famous but nobody knows who wrote it. Whoever it was must have been very close to God. It was written to show that even when we feel at our lowest, God is with us. Read it carefully. Think how God has been with you in times of trouble and of joy.

> One night I had a dream. I dreamed I was walking along the beach with God, and across the sky flashed scenes from my life. For each scene I noticed two sets of footprints in the sand, one belonged to me and the other to God.
>
> When the last scene of my life flashed before us I looked back at the footprints in the sand. I noticed that at times along the path of life there was only one set of footprints.
>
> I also noticed that it happened at the very lowest and saddest times of my

life. This really bothered me and I questioned God about it. 'God, you said that once I decided to follow you, you would walk with me all the way, but I noticed that during the most troublesome times in my life there is only one set of footprints. I don't understand why in times when I needed you most, you would leave me.'

God replied, 'My precious, precious child, I love you and I would never, never leave you during your times of trials and suffering. When you see only one set of footprints it was then that I carried you.'

Draw some of your own experiences when God might have carried you, as well as the times when he simply walked beside you. Or write your own poem showing how God is with us.

Trust walk

Do we trust our friends? If we can trust them, then how much more can we trust our loving Father who knows us so well? We learn to trust God as we know more about him. We worry about many things but if we trust God, we will know that he is there beside us even when times are hard. God does not promise that we will have *no* bad times, but he *does* promise that he will be with us through those hard times.

Try a trust game with a friend. In pairs blindfold one securely. One partner can direct the other or lead them around an obstacle course. Make your obstacle course with whatever is around: e.g. chairs — to go round; tables — to crawl under; steps — to climb, etc. Ask other friends to help by being 'obstacles'. e.g. making archways with arms or legs to climb over or under. Do not let the person who is blindfolded see your

obstacle course. He or she must rely completely on the person who is leading. He or she must *trust* his or her partner.

Some children are very frightened by being blindfolded. Do not attempt to use this game if that is the case, although it is worth talking about the fears and how we can trust each other — and God even more. Unfortunately, it is becoming more and more difficult to encourage trust — we are let down by other humans too often. It is worth considering:

- How do we lose trust in somebody?
- Are we totally trustworthy ourselves?
- How do we let each other down?

PRAYER AND PRAISE

Prayer sheet

You will need a piece of paper (A4) and a pencil each. Fold the paper into four. Draw a picture or symbol, or write a word in each of the four sections to show the following:

- something that you have seen today that makes you say 'Wow! Thank you God!'
- somebody or something that you want to bring before God
- something you have done for which you are sorry
- something that you see in the world or in you that you want God to change

When finished, the prayer sheets are collected in a bowl and offered to God. They are private and between God and those who have written or drawn them. Some people may prefer the prayer sheets to be burned.

My Prayer Sheet

25 Christ triumphant
34 Come and praise the Lord our King

137 Jesus is Lord!
139 Jesus' love is very wonderful

Twenty-six

SHAVUOT

INTRODUCTION

Shavuot is a Jewish festival. The Bible refers to this festival as Pentecost.

In the second chapter of the Acts of the Apostles we read that many Jews were in Jerusalem for the Festival of Pentecost (see session 27). The word Pentecost is made up from *pente* which means 'fifty'. There are fifty days after Passover until this festival. *Shavuot* is the Jewish word for 'weeks'. There are seven weeks (fifty days) after Passover until Shavuot.

The festival has many names and many reasons for celebrating: the Festival of giving the Torah (Hag Matan Torah), the Festival of First Fruits, and the Harvest Festival are just three. It is one of the three pilgrim festivals, when people were expected to try to get to the Temple in Jerusalem with their gifts. (Although there is no Temple now in Jerusalem, pilgrims still visit the Holy City when they can.)

In the past there was a great procession of pilgrims. It was led by an ox with horns painted gold and decorated with leaves. There were lots of musicians in the procession, with tambourines, flutes, etc. Everybody carried baskets decorated with leaves and flowers. In them they carried bread — baked from the first harvest of wheat — as well as the first ripened fruits: oranges,

grapefruit, lemons, with maybe grapes and dates. The Jewish name for the first fruits is *bikurim*.

The Torah refers to the Law that was given to the Israelites on Mount Sinai and by which they were expected to live. Some of these rules are very detailed and complex. The part with which we are most familiar is the Ten Commandments. We read about how Moses received those Commandments in the book of Exodus.

STORY

God gives his Laws
Exodus 19 and 20

ACTIVITIES

Rules for Today

The rules given to Moses were given for the people of that time — a nomadic tribe travelling around the desert. The rules covered how they were to live together in peace. There were even important rules about hygiene and food preparation.

When Jesus was asked about rules, he told his questioner that there were two important laws only. We usually hear those rules in the summary of the Law in Matthew 22:37-40: we should love God completely, and treat all people as well as we would like to be treated by them.

We all need to keep to certain rules or there would be chaos. If drivers decided that it did not matter which side of the road they drove on nobody would be safe. What rules do we have to live by?

- the law of the land?
- school rules?
- rules of the road — road safety?
- rules in our homes?
- God's rules?

Imagine that you and a group of friends are marooned on a desert island. To begin with you get on well, but as usual, after a time, you begin to quarrel amongst yourselves. Gradually you begin to realize that you have to decide on a set of rules by which you should live. What rules would you propose and how would you enforce them?

Do your rules have any similarity to the Ten Commandments and/or the summary of the Law which Jesus gave us? What rules (if any) do you need in whichever groups you belong to (e.g. Sunday club, school, family, church)?

The Ten Commandments

Make the two tablets of stone received by Moses from God on Mount Sinai. You can use clay — or simply represent the stone by strong card. The quick-drying clay is ideal for this, although it is inclined to crack when dry — hardboard or lino tiles make good surfaces to work on. Make sure there is somewhere flat where the clay can dry without being disturbed. Roll the clay out on a board like pastry. It will need to be about a centimetre thick. Use an old knife to trim off the edges into a good 'stone tablet' shape — maybe like an arched window. Don't forget that you will need two 'stones' and each will need to be quite large to fit on all the writing.

Use a defunct ballpoint pen to write the Commandments. A children's Bible may give you a simplified version of the Commandments, or you could write Jesus' summary of the Law. Mistakes can be wiped over with a damp cloth but it may be best to map out how the writing will go before you start to see how each Commandment will fit in. The writing will need to be big enough to be clear, but not too big, as there is quite a lot to get on.

Allow the clay to dry slowly and naturally. Do not attempt to move it until it is dry as it will almost certainly crack. Painting the finished and dry article with PVA glue will protect it and act like a varnish.

Bikurim basket

In Israel, the harvest at this time is of citrus fruits — oranges, lemons, grapefruit, etc. These don't grow in our country and most of our harvest is later in the year but there are usually soft fruits — strawberries, gooseberries, perhaps a few raspberries and blackcurrants. There may be beans, peas and early potatoes, and tomatoes and other salad items may be grown in greenhouses. At this time there are also flowers of many kinds.

Find a basket or punnet and decorate it with leaves and flowers. Place the harvest produce inside. Remember that summer fruits are soft and delicate: they need to be treated with care, with as little handling as possible.

The *bikurim* baskets may be carried in procession, along with the tablets showing the Ten Commandments or Jesus' summary of the Law. Singing should accompany the procession whilst the musical instruments are played. The *bikurim* baskets could be given to elderly, sick, lonely and/or housebound people later, or sold amongst the congregation and the money given to charity.

Shavuot procession

You will need *bikurim* baskets, the Commandment tablets and any musical instruments you can find or make, especially percussion instruments (see session 30). Sing some of the suggested hymns/songs as you go along and stop at a convenient place for some prayers.

PRAYER AND PRAISE

Leader: God is very good to us. Let us praise him!

All: God is very good to us. Let us praise him!

Leader: God who created this wonderful world

All: We thank you Lord, and praise your name.

Leader: God who gave us all that we need to eat

All: We thank you Lord, and praise your name.

Leader: God who gave us the first fruits of our harvest

All: We thank you Lord, and praise your name.

Leader: God who gave us rules by which to live

All: We thank you Lord, and praise your name.

Leader: Forgive us when we have wasted your gifts.

All: Forgive us Lord.

Leader: Forgive us when we have not shared our plenty.

All: Forgive us Lord.

Leader: Forgive us for when we have disobeyed your rules.

All: Forgive us Lord.

Leader: Help us to use those rules to share our plenty.

All: Help us Lord.

Leader: Help us to use those rules to make a happy, safe world.

All: Help us Lord. God is very good to us. Let us praise Him!

Shavuot Prayer

Blessed are you, O Lord our God, King of the universe, who has kept us in life, and preserved us, and enabled us to reach this season.

48 For the beauty of the earth
63 God who made the earth
276 When Israel was in Egypt's land
395 It takes an almighty hand
488 What colours God has made

Twenty-seven

PENTECOST

INTRODUCTION

The disciples really did go through a very difficult time. Their beloved friend and leader, after an exciting ride into Jerusalem when he was proclaimed King, was then arrested and in the most humiliating and unfair trial was condemned to die. He had even been betrayed by one of them — Judas. The rest of them must have felt guilt mixed with their own fear when they ran away to save themselves. The horrific death of Jesus on the cross must have been so hard to bear.

Yet, three days later, Jesus was alive again. Those must have been such happy days, when they were able to talk with Jesus again. When you have lost something very special to you, you love it even more when you have it back. This is the same with people, and the disciples must have hoped that Jesus would never leave them again. Jesus knew this was not possible. If he was to be with them all as they set off on their different journeys, Jesus would have to change from the man he was and leave them. However, he would never leave them completely for he would send a helper — the Spirit of God.

STORY

The Spirit comes to the Apostles
Acts 2:1-11
The adventure begins (p. 190)

ACTIVITIES

This is the Church's birthday, for at Pentecost the Church began. The disciples of Jesus were able to start their work of telling others about Jesus.

Birthday cake
Make or buy a plain cake. A Victoria sponge is probably a good choice. You will need a stiff icing sugar mixture or marzipan, with red and yellow food dyes. *Wash your hands.* Divide the mixture into several portions. Use the food dyes in different quantities and blends to make yellows, oranges and reds. Roll the mixture flat on a pastry board — dusting with icing sugar. Cut out flame shapes or simply mould with *clean* fingers. Arrange these around the base of the cake. Place a large candle or a number of small candles on the top.

If there is nowhere clear to work, a card collar could be put around the cake with flames — cut from tissue or crêpe paper — stuck to the collar.

When blowing out the candle/candles or

cutting the cake, a blessing could be said:

> Spirit of God, we welcome you like the disciples did. We thank you for your presence with us at all times. Spirit of the living God, be with us always to help us as we tell others of your love.

Hand-held windmill

At Pentecost the Holy Spirit came in wind and fire so we often use images of wind and fire to remind us of the work of the Holy Spirit.

You will need:
- *square of coloured paper or thin card*
- *scissors*
- *drawing pin*
- *piece of dowelling or garden cane*

Make diagonal cuts as shown in the diagram. Fold over the corners as shown and secure in the middle with the drawing pin. Pin the windmill to the dowelling or cane.

Doves and flames mobile

You will need:
- *orange, red and yellow card (or plain card painted)*
- *scissors*
- *thin white card*
- *wire coat hangers*
- *thread*

Fold and cut the doves from the thin white card as shown. Find the 'centre of gravity' for each dove. this is where you can hold the dove lightly between finger and thumb and it will not tip over backwards or forwards. You will probably find it about where the circle is, near the eye on the diagram. Attach thread to the dove at this point and tie to the coat hanger. It should balance well.

Cut flames from the coloured card. If you are using painted card from cereal packets, add PVA (white glue) to the paint so that it will stick without flaking. Find the centre of gravity like the dove and attach with thread to the coat hanger.

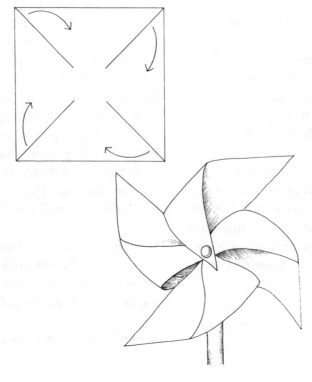

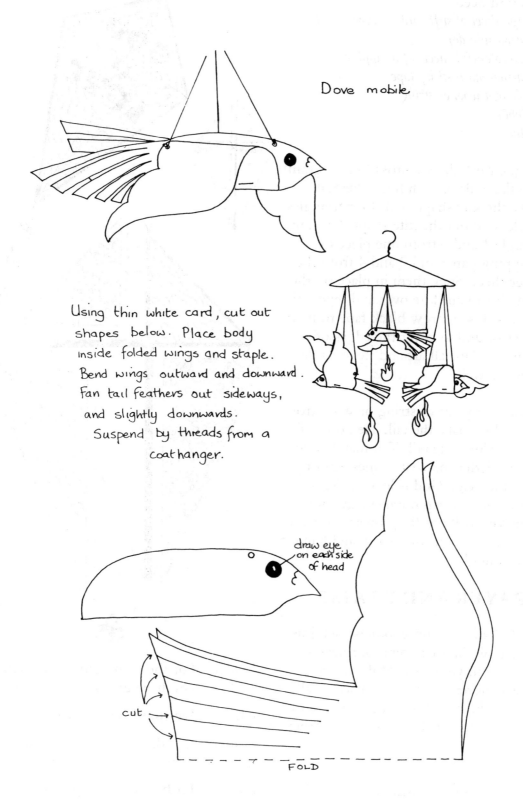

Dove mobile

Using thin white card, cut out
shapes below. Place body
inside folded wings and staple.
Bend wings outward and downward.
Fan tail feathers out sideways,
and slightly downwards.
   Suspend by threads from a
   coathanger.

draw eye
on each side
of head

cut

FOLD

Pentecost kites

You will need:

- *large sheet of stiff card (a large cereal carton will do)*
- *two colourful sheets of wrapping paper*
- *narrow black sticky tape*
- *coloured wool or string*
- *ribbon*
- *glue*

On the card, draw a cross (see diagram). Join the ends of each line. This will make the kite shape with four triangles inside. Cut out the kite shape. Cut out triangle 1 and 3 from one piece of wrapping paper and 2 and 4 from the other sheet. Stick them in place on the card. Turn your kite over and repeat the process. Use narrow black tape to mark the cross and to cover the edges of the triangles. Tape all around the outside edges as well.

Tie a long piece of string or wool from the end to make the tail. Tie bows of ribbon along the tail. You may like to cut out letters or write a message on your kite: e.g. 'God is love' or 'Come Holy Spirit'. Keep the message short. Your kite will not fly properly so tie a piece of string from the top and hang it from a hook.

PRAYER AND PRAISE

God of all love and goodness, send us your Holy Spirit to bind our hearts together in your love. Make us truly your children, brothers and sisters all around the world with the courage to use our gifts for the good of all. Amen.

Leader   God is good!

All   Let us praise him!

Leader   Come Holy Spirit,

All   Come and be with us now.

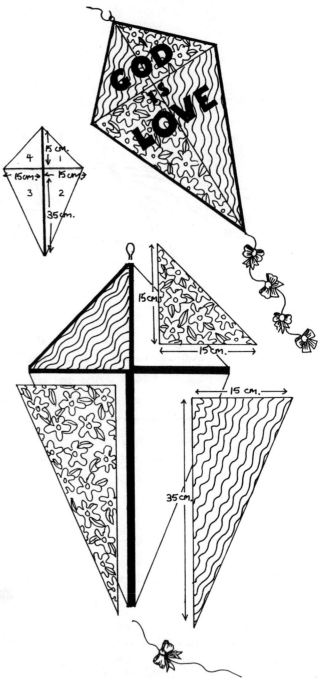

Leader   For the many gifts and talents you have given us:

All   We thank you Lord.

Leader   For all those who think they have no gifts or talents:

All   Holy Spirit, help us to discover our gifts.

Leader   For all those who wish to use their gifts more:

All	**Holy Spirit, help us explore the possibilities.**	5	**All over the world**
Leader	For all teachers and those who learn from them:	47	**For I'm building a people of power**
All	**Be with them in their work.**	62	**God whose Son (When the Spirit came)**
Leader	For all those who share the 'Good News' with others:	409	**Jesus, send me the helper**
All	**Give us the courage to speak out.**	465	**Spirit of God, please fill me**

Twenty-eight

TRINITY

INTRODUCTION

Trinity Sunday is the name given to the Sunday after Pentecost. It used to be the start of a long season in the Church called Trinity. In some churches this is still so but in others the season is now called Pentecost, starting a week before.

Trinity is a difficult word to explain. To put it as simply as possible, it refers to how there is just *one* God but we recognize him in three ways. ('Tri' means three — as in triangle, tricycle, etc.) St Patrick suggested that the Trinity is like a shamrock leaf (see session 7). A shamrock is like a clover leaf: it is one leaf but there are three parts. The following illustration is perhaps even more helpful.

You will need:
- *kettle (and power point)*
- *tray*
- *clear plastic bag*
- *jug of water*
- *ice cubes*
- *enough cups for each person*
- *bowl or large jug to collect water*
- *plastic sheet on floor*

Give each person a sip of water. What are you drinking? It is very important to our lives: we cannot do without water. Touch, feel and describe the water. What does it feel like?

Give each person an ice cube. What is that? Hold, feel and describe the ice: e.g. hard, cold. We need ice. Why? — refrigeration — storage of food. As the ice melts, what does it become?

Put the remaining water and ice into the kettle. *In a safe place* plug in the kettle and leave the water to boil. Whilst the water is heating, talk about the many uses of water and ice: drinking, washing, floating, sanitation, lubrication, painting, etc.

When the water starts to boil you will see a cloud coming out of the spout. What is the cloud coming out of the spout? (*steam*). Hold the plastic bag open, *carefully*, near the spout. *It is very important that an adult does this as it can burn.* The steam should condense on the inside of the bag and revert to water.

What is special about the water, ice and steam? It is the same thing, in different forms. The chemical formula (special name) is H_2O. H_2O is water, ice and steam, but each of those three is quite different. It is very difficult to explain and understand but think of God rather like the water, ice and steam. To make it easier, we call each part or form of God by a different name — God the Father (or Creator), God the Son (Jesus) and God the Holy Spirit — but they are all one God, just like the water, ice and steam are H_2O in different forms.

ACTIVITIES

Trinity triangle

Use a pencil, ruler and compass to make an equilateral triangle (one with sides of equal length). On a piece of stiff paper or card draw a line near one edge. Put the point of the compass at one end of the line and the pencil end at the other. Make an arc with the compass. Reverse the compass and pencil points and make another arc. The point where the arcs meet is where the other two sides of the triangle should reach. Cut out the triangle. Join the points mid-way along each side to make four smaller triangles (see diagram). Fold along these lines.

Write in the words as shown in the diagram. Each section could be illustrated with ways in which we see that part of God:

- the Father — Creator. God made the world so that section could show God's wonderful world of creation.
- the Son — Jesus the Pattern. Jesus came to live on the earth as a human to show us how God wants us to live. Events from his life and some of his teachings could be illustrated in this section.

- the Holy Spirit — God living in people today. The Holy Spirit helps us to do God's will in the world. Draw or cut out from newspapers or magazines pictures of people who are working for God in different ways.

Trinity circle

The same idea can be done in a circle. You will need three circles. The first should be as big as possible with the other two fitting inside (see diagram). On the top, smallest circle, draw, paint or cut out from different materials to make plants, animals, insects, birds, fish, etc. Around the outside of the second circle draw events from the life of Jesus along with some of his teachings, e.g. the Lord's Prayer, the parables (Good Samaritan). On the last, outer circle, draw or cut out pictures from magazines and newspapers showing people working with the help of the Holy Spirit — God working through us.

The circles may be fastened together with a split-pin fastener in the middle. Join all the circles by making stems of leaves from string and paper 'leaves' stuck or stitched to the string. Make six or seven strings and attach them to the centre and the outside edge.

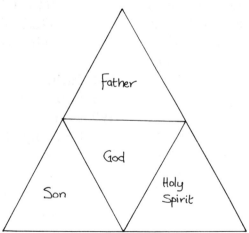

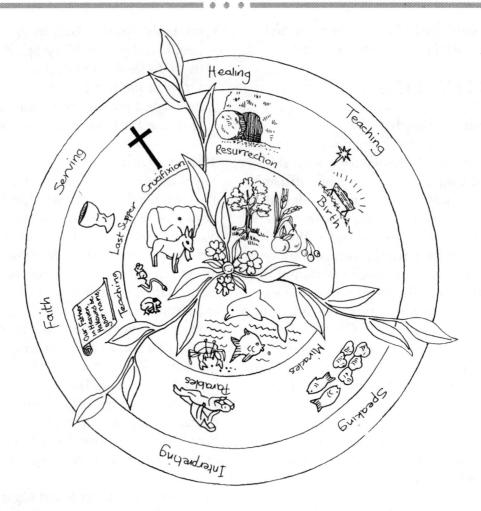

PRAYER AND PRAISE

Leader 1: I bring this flower as a sign to remind me of my God: God the Father, Creator, who made the world and all that is in it.

A flower is placed on the altar.

Leader 2: I bring this cross as a sign to remind me of my God: God the Son, Jesus, who saved the world and died on a cross for me.

A cross is placed on the altar.

Leader 3: I bring this candle, the flame of which reminds me of my God: God the Holy Spirit, who lives inside me and helps me to know your will.

A lighted candle is placed on the altar.

All: We have three things to remind us of our God:
God the Trinity,
God who made us,
God who saved us,
God who lives in us,
The One in Three and Three in One,
The Trinity,
God of love, God who is with us always. Amen.

  44 Father, we adore you
  45 Father we love you
199 Praise God from whom all blessings flow
268 We really want to thank you Lord
392 I'm going to shine, shine, shine
455 Sing praise to God the Father

Twenty-nine

ST PETER

INTRODUCTION

St Peter's Day is 29 June. Many churches are dedicated (named after) St Peter. What do we know about him? The gospels of Matthew, Mark, Luke and John tell us quite a lot. In fact, Peter may have helped Mark in compiling his gospel. The book called the Acts of the Apostles (generally shortened to 'Acts') gives information about Peter's life after Jesus ascended.

Matthew 4:18-20 tells how Peter was one of the first disciples, along with his brother Andrew and two other men who were brothers, James and John. That same passage tells that all these men were fishermen, working on Lake Galilee. Peter lived in Capernaum, a small town on the shores of Lake Galilee. He had a wife and a mother-in-law whom Jesus healed (Mark 1:29-31).

Peter was one of the closest friends of Jesus and was with him for several important events (Mark 5:21-42, especially verse 37 — the healing of Jairus' daughter, and Matthew 17:1-9 — the Transfiguration). It was Peter who saw that Jesus was so special and was the Son of God and he said so.

When Jesus washed the feet of the disciples during the Last Supper, Peter tried to stop him. He hated to see his

Master doing the task of a slave, but Jesus explained that we must all serve each other (John 13:3-9). Peter was with Jesus in the Garden of Gethsemane when he was arrested. He had a sword with him and tried to stop the guards from taking Jesus away. He cut off a servant's ear but Jesus did not want this, and he stopped Peter and healed the servant (John 18:10-11).

It was after this that Peter did something terrible that he would remember all his life. When Jesus was in dreadful trouble and especially needed his friends with him, Peter let him down. He even said that he did not know Jesus. All the gospels tell this story. In Jerusalem on the place where it happened, there is a church (one of hundreds in the city). This church is often called 'Cock Crow' after the cock that crowed, reminding Peter of what

Jesus had said: 'Before the cock crows, you will say you don't know me three times'.

Peter was evidently rather impulsive, (that means he said the first thing that came into his head), but Jesus recognized that Peter was a good, strong leader and was very dependable. Jesus even had a nickname for Peter. Peter was not his real name — it was Simon — but Jesus called him Peter which means 'rock'. Rocks are good strong substances that we can build on. Jesus said that he would build his Church on Peter — Peter would be the first to tell people about Jesus and so his Church would be started.

STORY

Peter denies knowing Jesus
Matthew 26:31-35; 69-75
Soldiers in the night (p. 182)

In spite of this denial, Jesus made a special point of seeing Peter after his resurrection. At a breakfast near the lake, he asked Peter to lead his followers like a shepherd leads his sheep (John 21:15-19).

Peter and the other disciples were there when Jesus returned to heaven — the Ascension (Acts 1:9-11). Ten days later, on the day of Pentecost when the Holy Spirit had come to them, it was Peter who spoke to the crowds and told them bravely all about Jesus (Acts 2). There are many other stories about Peter in the Acts of the Apostles. He was arrested and put in prison but God let him out; he healed a sick man at the Beautiful Gate to the city of Jerusalem; he had a strange dream that told him that God wanted him to preach to people who were not Jews and not just to Jews as the disciples thought God wanted.

Peter wrote at least two important letters (called epistles) which are found in the New Testament. The rest of Peter's life is *not* told in the Bible. The Christians were persecuted under the Romans: thousands were tortured and killed when they refused to give up their faith. It is probable that Peter died in Rome. It is said that he was crucified. Peter said that he was not good enough to die in the same way that Jesus had died. Although it was, if possible, an even more cruel and slow death, Peter instead asked to be crucified upside-down, so that he could look up towards heaven.

Pictures of Peter often show him holding keys in his hands. In Matthew 16:19 Jesus says, 'I will give you the keys of the kingdom of Heaven; what you forbid on earth shall be forbidden in Heaven and what you allow on earth shall be allowed in Heaven.'

ACTIVITIES

This is Your life
Use the information we find in the Bible, plus any more you can find, to make a *This is Your Life* album. Pretend to be the people who knew Peter and tell the stories about him, just like they do on the television. Try to make your stories as interesting as possible. Really think what you would have seen, how you would have felt, and why you have remembered so clearly. You will need a

large red folder in which to keep all the information. Draw some pictures to illustrate your stories.

Stained glass windows

Gloucester Cathedral is one of the many churches which are dedicated to St Peter. There is a very large window there that tells the story of St Peter. In it there are scenes showing many events from his life. Make your own picture, or series of pictures, to make up a large stained glass window. You could use certain symbols and items that were important in his life, such as the cock, keys, a boat, fish, an upside down cross.

The stained glass windows can be made from a 'tissue sandwich' (see session 15, Candlemas). Alternatively, you can use ordinary felt pens on kitchen paper (or similar). The window 'panes' can be painted with cooking oil, which makes the paper transparent. This can be rather messy and should not be left up in a window too long as it will form an oily crust which is *very difficult to remove!*

Ballad of St Peter

A ballad is a song or poem that tells a story. Write a poem or song about St Peter, or part of his story. Use a favourite song tune or, if you are really clever, make up your own music. It will need to match the mood of the story.

Try to feel how the people in the story felt. You could pretend to be Peter himself and perhaps tell how you felt when you let down Jesus. 'Peter's Denial' from *Jerusalem Joy* by Roger Jones and 'Bitter was the night' by Sydney Carter may give you ideas.

Following on from Peter

The first Christians went out and told others about Jesus. They met regularly to learn more and to thank God for his love. Peter and the other disciples could not do all the work themselves. They chose good men to act as deacons. St Stephen, whose feast is on Boxing Day, was one of the first deacons.

The leaders of the Church, the Apostles (Peter and the other eleven), laid their hands on the deacons. On the feast of St Peter all over the country leaders in the Church (bishops) will lay their hands on men and women just as the Apostles did to the first deacons. Many deacons become priests and a few priests become bishops. They in their turn lay hands on deacons and ordain priests (the same process of laying on of hands).

All through the ages the authority of the Church has been passed on by the laying on of hands, right from the Apostles to the present day. This is referred to as the 'Apostolic Succession'. Some churches feel this is very important. Other churches do not like the idea and have abandoned it.

PRAYER AND PRAISE

Pray for those ordained priest and made deacon at this time and for all clergy, ministers and leaders of the Church. You may use the collect for St Peter's Day — 29 June — which is found in some prayer books.

Leader	Let us thank God for the life and example of St Peter.
All	**Thank you, God.**
Leader	Jesus, you called Peter to do many things that he did not expect.
All	**Help us to hear and come when you say 'Follow me'.**
Leader	Let us say a prayer for those who need to be remembered today; those who have made the news headlines today because of what they have said or done:
All	**Lord, bless them and be with them.**
Leader	Those who speak out for right and those who fear to speak out because of what others may think or do:
All	**Lord, bless them and be with them.**
Leader	Those we have met today; those we knew and those who were strangers:
All	**Lord, bless them and be with them.**

Leader	Those who do not know *you*, Lord:
All	**Lord, bless them and be with them.**
Leader	Those who will help others to know you:
All	**Lord, bless them and be with them.**
Leader	Those who are beginning their lives as deacons and priests:
All	**Lord, bless them and be with them.**
Leader	All of us who try to do God's will, like St Peter:
All	**Lord, bless us and be with us.**

16 **Big man standing**
197 **Peter and James and John**
198 **Peter and John went to pray**
286 **Who took fish and bread**
397 **It was Jesus who taught his disciples**
451 **See the man walking**
Jerusalem Joy:
Listen Peter, do you know him?
English Praise:
Bitter was the night

Thirty

MUSIC

INTRODUCTION

Music is very special. It can make us think about sad things or it can make us very happy or excited. Music can express all sorts of feelings. When we are happy we can hardly stop ourselves from singing. A mother may sing a lullaby to soothe her baby to sleep. We use music to tell stories. We hear music all the time as we go about our lives.

Experts have realized the importance of music. Farmers sometimes play music as they milk their cows so that they keep still and calm. Music is played endlessly in the shops to make the shoppers stay longer and buy more. In busy railway stations they will sometimes play fast, busy music that makes the people move faster. When they want the passengers to slow down they will play softer, slower music.

Most of us would find it a very sad world if there wasn't any music. There are lots of different kinds of music — pop music, classical music, hymns and songs, jazz, country, etc.

What is your favourite type of music? Most of us prefer one kind of music to another. We can listen to music or join in by making music ourselves. We may use our voices to make music or we may be lucky enough to be able to play a musical instrument.

St Cecilia is known as the Patron Saint of music. Not much is known about Cecilia, and most of that is legend but she lived in the second or third century AD in Rome. She was martyred rather than give up her faith and it is said that on her death she was taken up to Heaven holding a harp. Pictures show her like this.

STORY

David, the shepherd boy who killed the giant and later became King of Israel, was a musician. He played the harp to soothe King Saul when he was in one of his rages. He danced and sang before the Lord to show how happy he was that God loved him. There are 150 psalms or songs in the Bible. Many of them are said to have been written by David. Some of these psalms talk about singing and praising God with musical instruments.

Psalm 150

ACTIVITIES

Percussion instruments

Most of us are not clever enough to make musical instruments that play a tune. It takes years of practice to learn those skills, but you can make instruments that play the rhythm. There are lots of ways to make percussion instruments. Here are just a few:

Home-Made Percussion Instruments

dried beans in a yoghurt pot with a lid or tape over the top

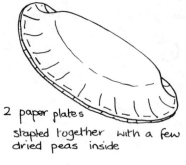

2 paper plates stapled together with a few dried peas inside

lentils rice pasta shapes

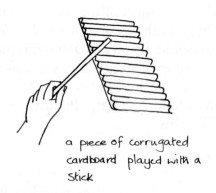

a piece of corrugated cardboard played with a stick

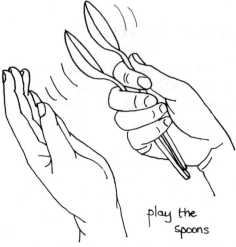

play the spoons

Psalm 150 banner

You will need:
- *a large piece of fabric, paper or card*
- *needle and thread*
- *scrap materials*
- *scissors*
- *PVA or similar glue*
- *pictures of musical instruments*
- *two pieces of thin wood to make a T shape*
- *drawing pins*

Fold and hem the edges of the background fabric to make neat edges. Look at the pictures of musical instruments and copy their shapes onto your scrap material. Cut them out and stick them onto the background. Arrange the pictures of instruments to make sure that the whole collage makes a pleasing picture. Pin or stick the banner along the top of the T.

Favourite hymns

You may enjoy finding out the favourite hymns in your church. Ask everybody to write down their favourite hymn and why it is their favourite. When you have everybody's choice, you can put them all together and see which hymns most people chose. Organize a *Songs of Praise* service to sing the favourites, and get people to tell why they made those choices.

Jubilate dance

The music to 'Jubilate' (*Junior Praise* 145) has the kind of music familiar in Israel. You can dance to it. Stand in a circle or a row, with hands on the shoulders of those on either side of you.

1. Put your left foot across in front of the right, bending your knees as you move.

2. Take a step to the right with right foot.
3. Put your left foot across and behind the right.
4. Repeat 2.

Repeat these four steps as you move round. Sometimes it helps to start slowly and gradually get faster. Don't get out of breath! It is much easier to do than describe.

You may need help with the singing from those who are not dancing. They can clap their hands in time with the music. Other good dance songs are:

408 Jesus put this song into our hearts
481 This is a catchy songa (The Christian Conga)

PRAYER AND PRAISE

Obviously, most of this section could be music. You could sing the Caribbean version of the Lord's Prayer (*Junior Praise* 192) and sing Psalm 150. Use your percussion instruments to accompany your favourite hymns or play whatever musical instrument you can.

Thank you, Lord, for the gift of music. Thank you for those who sing and play, and those who compose and arrange music. Thank you for all the different kinds of music — for our favourites and the favourites of others. Amen.

All: Praise the Lord for music.

Individuals or groups could say a line each:

Praise the Lord for composers and players.
Praise the Lord with shakers and scrapers.
Praise the Lord with drums and cymbals.
Praise the Lord with guitars and violins.
Praise the Lord with pianos and organs.
Praise the Lord with flutes and clarinets.
Praise the Lord with recorders and oboes.
Praise the Lord with trumpets and trombones.
Praise the Lord with tubas and cornets.
Praise the Lord with our voices, high and low, soft and loud.
Praise the Lord for singers and dancers.

All: Let everything that can make music praise the Lord!

145 Jubilate
192 Our Father who is in Heaven
200 Praise him on the trumpet
205 Praise to the Lord our God
398 It's a song of praise
408 Jesus put this song into our hearts
454 Sing a new song to the Lord
481 This is a catchy songa (The Christian Conga)

Thirty-one

GARDENS AND FLOWERS

INTRODUCTION

Times of celebration or remembrance are often marked with flowers. Flowers help to decorate a place; they cheer us when we are feeling sad; and add colour and joy to a happy occasion. Have you ever given flowers to somebody you love? Watch anybody's face when he or she is given flowers. You will almost certainly see great pleasure and joy in that face. Flowers have that effect on most of us, rather like music.

Most of us try to have flowers around us at least sometimes. Many of us are lucky enough to have gardens where we can watch flowers at their very best. Those who do not have gardens probably try to have potted plants in the house or window boxes full of colourful flowers. We can all enjoy parks and gardens around us. We use the senses of sight, smell, touch and even taste when we enjoy flowers and plants.

Traditionally, flowers have been given special meanings. People in the past would give flowers which convey a message.

- rosemary — remembrance
- forget—me—not — don't forget me!
- rhododendron — danger!
- iris — I have a message for you

We still use the 'language of flowers' today. For instance, many people will plant rosemary on graves or put it in wreaths. This signifies that they will always remember the person who has died. Red roses are often used as a sign of love for another. There is a beautiful lily called a Madonna lily. This is often used to remember Mary, the mother of Jesus. (Nothing to do with the singer!) Pictures of Mary are often shown with her carrying the lily in her hand.

Flowers look beautiful wherever they are, but we often like to arrange them in vases in our homes and of course in our churches. Week after week, thousands of people all over the world give their time and skill, in love, to decorate and make beautiful their church. It is their way of showing how much they want to praise God. Many churches use the fact that flowers are so special to have a flower festival. It may take weeks or months to prepare but it will be worth it, for many people will have the opportunity to enjoy really beautiful flowers.

Jesus loved flowers. He took note of what he called 'lilies of the field'. These may have been any wild flowers or perhaps particularly the anemones — reds, blues and purples — that grow all over the hillsides of Galilee. Jesus was telling us not to worry, because God cares about us so much. He cares for the wild flowers. If God cares for the wild flowers as much as he does, how much more will he care for us, his children?

STORY

Consider the lilies of the field
Luke 12:27–31

Look at the wild flowers. See how they grow. They don't work or make clothes for themselves. But I tell you that even Solomon, the great and rich king, was not dressed as beautifully as one of these flowers.

ACTIVITIES

Herb garden

Monks living in monasteries and abbeys used to grow herbs. Herbs are plants of many kinds that have another use other than just decoration. Not only do they look good but they often smell wonderful and can be useful in lots of ways. Many are used for flavouring our food. Most people will have come across thyme, sage, rosemary and parsley. If you look in the cupboard at home you may find lots more.

In the past, herbs were also used extensively for healing. They are beginning to be used very much again now. Some experts consider them to be safer than most modern drugs. Another use for herbs is in the making of cosmetics and toiletries. There are lots of interesting books about herbs and herb gardens. Also books about monks and their lives often mention the growing of herbs for healing and cooking.

You may like to make your own herb garden. Many gardeners grow a few herbs (even if they do not use them). You may be able to beg a few cuttings, e.g. lavender, rosemary, thyme, sage, mint — all of these grow freely and may be cut without fear of damaging the plants. Arrange them in a geometric design in a seed tray of soil or sand and water them well. Some may take root and should then be transferred to larger pots or the garden. Alternatively, you can buy small herb plants quite cheaply. These could be planted as a group in a small patch, perhaps in the church grounds where they may be enjoyed by all — not only for their beauty but for their wonderful perfume.

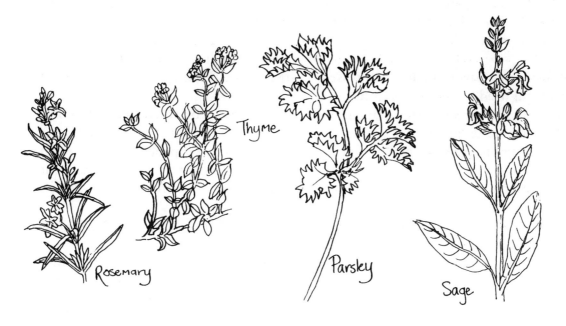

Pot-pourri

Herbs may be used to make a *pot-pourri*. Collect a few bits of herb — any that smell nice will do — and put the leaves and flowers into a bowl. They will keep a room smelling good for a long time. Alternatively, you could fill circles of material with herbs such as lavender. Tie them into little bundles with ribbon or wool and put them amongst bedding and clothes to make them smell sweet. A small pillow filled with herbs is said to help you sleep.

Flower arrangement

Arrange flowers in a vase. The use of 'oasis' (a sponge-like material which holds the water) makes it much easier. Make sure that all the flowers can reach the water. Try to blend your colours carefully, although God's colour schemes never seem to clash. As a general rule, it is best to keep bright coloured flowers and those with large heads in the middle whilst lighter shades and small heads can go around the edges. However, your arrangement can be just as you want it.

Very small children may find it easier to use flower heads in a sand tray (seed tray) to make a pattern like a hassock (kneeler). The whole tray will need to be covered with the flowers.

Flowers and leaves can also be pressed (this will need to be done well in advance) and used to make a picture. It requires nimble fingers and it often helps to use tweezers to pick up the flowers as they stick to fingers. Arrange them on a piece of coloured paper or card that reflects the colours of your flowers. Stick them with a tiny spot of glue. They may look very good in a frame.

Miniature garden

Design your own miniature garden in a seed tray. Bits of heather or fir make good 'trees'. You could even have a pond in your garden (a small mirror or piece of silver foil). Make sure the soil covers the edges. You may be able to find some moss for the grass, but if you can't get that, mix sawdust in green powder paint and sprinkle it over the earth/sand.

Would your garden be a place where you would like to spend your time if you were small enough?

Seasonal garden picture

Flowers and all plants depend very much on the passing seasons for their growth. Many die back in the autumn and appear to 'sleep' through the winter, but begin to grow again in the spring. Each season has different plants growing. Make a garden picture showing the different seasons. In spring the predominant (main) colours are yellows and pale greens coming out of the brown earth. In summer there is a mixture of all colours, with perhaps pinks, purples and blues in dark green foliage (leaves). In autumn the leaves change to oranges, reds and browns and the fruits show red and black. In winter there are not so many colours — rather grey and white. The evergreens create the only colours.

All these can be re-created with collage material — fabrics of many kinds; crêpe, tissue and sugar paper; plus any natural material that can be gathered without damaging the environment.

PRAYER AND PRAISE

Leader   Praise the God of Creation,

All   Praise his holy name.

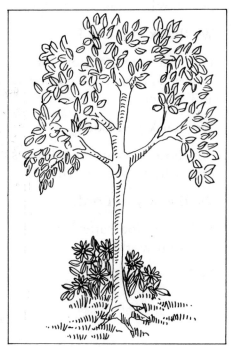
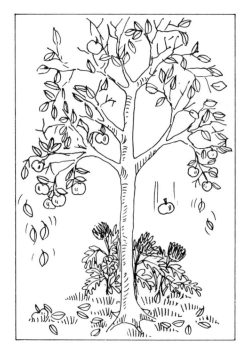
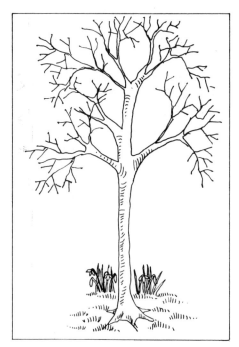

Leader   For the beauty of the flowers:

All   **We thank you Lord.**

Leader   For the pleasure and comfort that flowers give:

All   **We thank you Lord.**

Leader   For the healing powers of your plants:

All   **We thank you Lord.**

Leader   For those who use herbs to heal and soothe:

All   **We thank you Lord.**

Leader   For the flavour the flowers and herbs give to our food:

All   **We thank you Lord.**

Leader | For all who cook and feed us:

All | **We thank you Lord.**

Leader: | For all those who grow the flowers and plants — gardeners and farmers:

All | **We thank you Lord.**

Leader | For those who arrange flowers, especially in our churches:

All | **We thank you Lord.**

Leader | Help us to look after your beautiful world.

All | **Help us Lord.**

Leader | May we never destroy the beauty around us.

All | **Show us the way. Praise the God of Creation. Amen.**

6 **All things bright and beautiful**
48 **For the beauty of the earth**
254 **Think of a world without any flowers**
288 **Who put the colours in the rainbow?**
328 **Don't know much (This is God's world)**
347 **God in his love for us**
488 **What colours God has made**

Thirty-two

WINNING AND LOSING

INTRODUCTION

In the summer months in particular, thousands of young people go around with worried expressions. They snap at their friends and quarrel with parents. It is the time for exams and the pressure of trying to pass them can cause even the strongest and cleverest person to crumble! Competition does not end with exams however. We are tested in many ways all through our lives.

Adults compete to be the best so that they can get a good job. Politicians will win or lose elections. A politician will have spent weeks or even months canvassing — visiting people to try and persuade them to vote for him or her. At the election he or she has to wait to see if the voters have chosen him/her or somebody else. Explorers compete to be the first to reach some remote spot; the fastest to travel, or the one to cover the longest journey without help. Athletes compete to be the first: the fastest runner, the highest jumper, the longest thrower, the strongest lifter.

Schools often have Sports Day when nearly everybody competes. Not *all* of us are good at sports, and anyway only one person can win a race. We probably all know what it is like to win something. We may be unable to express *how* we feel but the feeling is good. We probably know what it is like to lose as well. This is usually not a good feeling. We may be very disappointed.

If we want to win in anything, we have to work hard. We must practise and practise and try our best. Whether we are learning to speak, read, to play a musical instrument or to drive a car, we have to practise or we will never be any good. When we do tests or take exams we need to learn the information and keep learning and re-learning — practise and more practise.

But we are not all good at the same things. Some of us feel that we are not good at anything. In school we may find work very difficult and everybody seems to be much cleverer than us. People may judge us by how clever we are but *God does not*. God knows that we are all different — he made us! God knows that we do not have to be clever or brainy to be kind and helpful to each other. To God, a loving smile is much more important than solving a difficult sum. Remember the story of the sheep and the goats — 'If you have done something good for anybody else, you have done it for me.'

However, God has given us all gifts, in whatever form, and he wants us to put them to the best use. Jesus told a story about using the good things we have.

STORY

The parable of the talents
Matthew 25:14-30

There is a man who is very good at running and has won many races. He is Kriss Akabussi. He knows how it feels to win but he also knows how it feels to lose. Kriss is a Christian and wherever he goes he tries to tell others about Jesus and his love for everybody. Kriss always has a smile for everybody; he cares for others. He knows that whatever he does, God loves him. He may be disappointed to lose a race but he will not let it get him down, as he knows he has tried his best and it hasn't changed God's love for him.

ACTIVITIES

Picnic and church games

Organize your own picnic and Sports Day. Races need to be varied enough so that those who are not athletic can still enjoy the games. Races which involve dressing up or carrying something carefully, three-legged races, sack races and wheelbarrow races are fun to most people. A good atmosphere of fun is what is most important.

You could make up games with a biblical theme, e.g. The Good Samaritan stakes. All the characters from the story can take part — robbers, a few other travellers, the priest, the Levite and the Samaritan. Of course, the Samaritan will come last as he has to stop to help the injured man, but he wins because of what he has done.

Winners' badges

With God we are all winners because he loves us so much. We can all wear a winner's badge.
You will need:
- *10 cm. disc of stiff card*
- *2 cm. strip of crêpe paper — cut across the pad*
- *glue*
- *safety pin and sticky tape*
- *felt pen*

On the disc, write a caption and/or draw a smiley face. Pleat the crêpe paper and stick it around the back of the outside edge of the disc. Stick the fixed part of the safety pin on the back of the card with sticky tape.

PRAYER AND PRAISE

God of Creation, we thank you for all those who use their imagination and skill to help us to see your wonderful world.

Lord Jesus, you were tested and tried: bless those who are going through difficult times. Bless them and give

them the courage to overcome their difficulties.

Spirit of the living God, help us to learn from those who, filled with your power, show your love in winning and losing. Amen.

42 **Father, I place into your hands**
98 **I have decided to follow Jesus**
108 **In our work and in our play**
429 **Maybe you can't draw or sing**
496 **When you're feeling good**

Thirty-three

ANIMALS

INTRODUCTION

Many of us own and love pets. You may have a dog or a cat; you may have goldfish, budgies or gerbils. You may have something really unusual. You may live on a farm with lots of animals. You may not have any pets at all and may only see animals on the television, in books or at the zoo. Whether it is the friendly dog that we take for walks and pat and stroke, the cow in the field, or the bird that flies in the sky above the motorway as we speed past in the car, God made these lovely creatures and he asks us to care for them and love them.

One of the best loved stories in the Bible is about a man, his family and lots of animals.

STORY

Noah and the ark
Genesis 7 and 8
A boat full of animals (p. 13)

ACTIVITIES

Folded card animals
You will need:
- *plenty of card*
- *felt pens or crayons*
- *scissors*
- *pictures of animals like those illustrated*
- *glue (to stick ears, etc.)*

Fold the card in half. On one side draw the animal or copy those illustrated. Make sure that the shape is simple and bold. The back of the animal must be straight as it will have to go along the fold of the card. Keep the card folded and cut around the animal shape. When the card is opened out, the animal will be able to stand on four legs. Colour both sides of the animal with felt pens or crayons.

Ark with animals
You will need:
- *a large cereal box*
- *smaller cereal box*
- *paint mixed with a little PVA glue*
- *card*
- *felt pens*
- *scissors*
- *two lollipop sticks*
- *glue*
- *kitchen roll tube*

Cut the large cereal box in half. Cut and fold in the sides of the box so that it becomes 'boat' shaped. Cut the other, smaller box in half lengthways. Make the roof from the other side of this box. Glue on the roof to the smaller box.

Cut doors in the smaller box. In the larger box that forms the base of the ark, cut holes on both sides that are just the diameter of the kitchen roll tube. Push the tube carefully through both

holes. Push the two lollipop sticks through the kitchen roll tube so that they lie at right angles to the tube (see diagram overleaf). Fix the smaller box over the larger to make the cabin of the ark.

Draw and cut out from card the animals as illustrated (or your own animals) and attach them to the ends of the lollipop sticks. As the kitchen roll tube is turned, the animals will appear in the doorway of the cabin. Mix a little PVA glue with some paint so that it will stick to the shiny surface of the cereal box and paint the whole of the outside of your ark.

You could place the folded animals from the first activity in twos in front of the

Noah's Ark

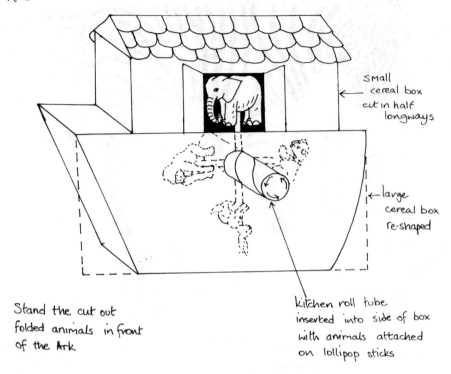

Small cereal box cut in half longways

large cereal box re-shaped

Stand the cut out folded animals in front of the Ark

kitchen roll tube inserted into side of box with animals attached on lollipop sticks

ark. You may like to make Noah and his wife and family from card and stick then in the ark too.

Noah and the animals music

Of course we cannot make living, moving animals like God, but we can make some fun animal masks like those in session 2. The *Carnival of the Animals* by Saint Saens can be used to tell the story of Noah and his ark full of animals. Wear the animal masks when you pretend to be the animals. One of the pieces from *Carnival of the Animals* is for the lion. He roars loudly in the music.

PRAYER AND PRAISE

You may be allowed to bring your pets to your church to be blessed. You must ask permission, as animals can make a mess and some people do not like them in church anyway. If this is allowed, you must make sure that you control the animals. Never bring animals that may be aggressive or those that frighten anybody.

Heavenly Father who made us and made all the animals, thank you for all the joys that they bring us. Help us to care for them and never to hurt them by our selfishness. Amen.

Leader   For all the animals that live in our homes and give us love and pleasure:

All   Thank you, Lord.

Leader   For all those that live on farms and provide us with food and clothing:

All   Thank you, Lord.

Leader   For animals that live in the countryside — squirrels, rabbits, deer, badgers and foxes:

All   Thank you, Lord.

Leader   For animals that live in hot

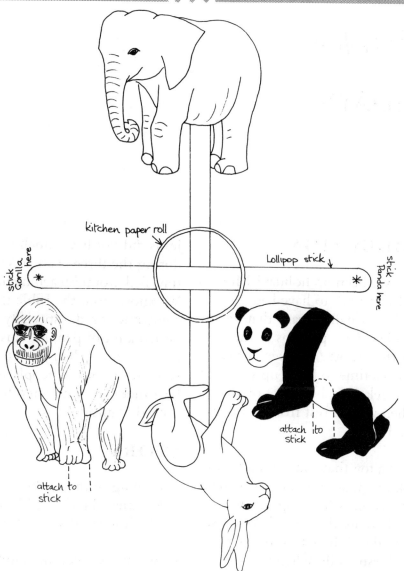

countries and in our zoos —
elephants, lions, tigers and
leopards:

All   **Thank you, Lord.**

Leader   For animals that live in the
seas — fish, seals, whales and
penguins:

All   **Thank you, Lord.**

Leader   For animals that fly in the air
— birds, butterflies, bugs and
beetles:

All   **Thank you, Lord.**

Leader   For animals that crawl on the
ground — snakes, frogs, slugs
and snails:

All   **Thank you, Lord.**

Leader   For all living creatures, large
and small, furry or hairy,
feathered or scaled, fierce or
gentle, wild or tame.

All   **Thank you, Lord.**

   6 All things bright and beautiful
167 Mister Noah built an ark
184 Oh, the Lord looked down
210 Rise and shine
288 Who put the colours in the
     rainbow?
432 Noah was the only good man
440 Old man Noah built an ark

Thirty-four

HOLIDAYS

INTRODUCTION

Have you ever been on holiday? Most of us are lucky enough to have had holidays. This usually means that we go away for a few days, perhaps to the seaside or the country, or even abroad. It is perhaps a time to catch up with old friends and relatives, but most of all it is a time when we can rest from our usual routine and relax.

If you have a toy that runs on batteries you will know that you have to change the batteries quite often, especially when you have used it a lot. Like those toys, we need our 'batteries' re-charged or changed, especially when we have been working hard. A holiday can act like new batteries for us — we feel refreshed and ready to start again. Parents can get very tired working very hard to keep their children fed and warm, safe and happy. They need a rest sometimes.

The word holiday comes from 'holy day'. This was traditionally the only time when people had time off. If you work on the land, or with animals in particular, you cannot just say you won't work for a few days. The animals have to be fed; the cows have to be milked *every* day.

Jesus did not have much time for rest during the three years in which he travelled around teaching and preaching. We know from the Bible that Jesus was sometimes tired, especially when he had healed a lot of people. This story tells of one occasion when Jesus tried to get some rest, but the people wanted to hear more from him and followed him onto the hillside.

STORY

Feeding of the 5,000
Matthew 14:13-21; Mark 6:30-42
The holiday that went wrong (p. 160)

In another gospel the number quoted is 4,000. Most of us are not very good at estimating numbers. All we *do* know is that there were a great many people at that picnic — too many to count.

ACTIVITIES

Picnic

This story is a good one to act out. You could have a real picnic, although obviously you will not be able to make it feed 5,000 people. Make it a sharing picnic. If everybody brings something there will be enough for everyone. Make sure that you do not leave any rubbish. Like the disciples, you can clear up any mess afterwards.

Holiday collage

Think of all the different kinds of holidays you might go on: seaside, country, abroad, London, farm, etc.; chalet, caravan, hotel, relations, etc.Make a big collage picture of all the kinds of holidays. Use scrap material and any other things, e.g. shells, leaves, etc.

Or, make a collection of postcards or photographs of holidays. Pin them up carefully as the owners will probably want them back. You may need to carefully write the owners' names on the back. Use pencil, very lightly.

PRAYER AND PRAISE

Bring in items that remind you of a good holiday — e.g. bucket and spade, photograph, present or souvenir, guidebook, etc. Try to get together a few symbols of happy times — as wide a variety as possible. Items could include shells, postcards, sun-cream, sun-hat, ice cream cone (just the cone — not the ice-cream!); bus, train or airline tickets, plus anything from the first list.

You may recall happy (or not so happy) events, people you met, friends you made, things you saw on your holidays. Holiday symbols can be placed on the altar (or table) with a few words, e.g. bucket and spade — Thank you for the sandcastle I made. There is no need for those who are shy to say anything. They may simply place their holiday symbol on the table in silence.

Leader   Lord Jesus, you know what it is to be tired. You were tired too.

All   Lord Jesus, be with us in our tiredness.

Leader   You tried to rest but everybody wanted you.

All   Lord Jesus, help us to understand everybody's need for rest and refreshment.

Leader   You give us strength in our weakness.

All   Lord Jesus, bless us and keep us.

Leader   You give us hope.

All   Lord Jesus, bless us and keep us.

Leader   You give us comfort and joy

All   Lord Jesus, bless us and keep us.

Leader   You give us healing of body and mind.

All   Lord Jesus, bless us and keep us and be with us now.

- 1 **A boy gave to Jesus**
- 26 **Clap your hands all you people**
- 108 **In our work and in our play**
- 118 **It's a happy day**
- 286 **Who took fish and bread**
- 403 **It's the little things**
- 408 **Jesus put this song into our hearts**
- 496 **When you're feeling good**

Thirty-five

LOOKING BACK AND MOVING ON

INTRODUCTION

End of term is a strange time. We are perhaps pleased that we are about to have a rest from work and routine, but most of us are lucky enough to really enjoy the work and being with friends (although we may not admit it!). So, some are sorry to finish the term. Many are perhaps sad because they will be leaving old friends and are rather nervous about going to a place where they do not know many people.

Growing up involves a lot of changes. We are constantly learning more and more. We meet new people and new situations, we learn new skills as well as facts. There is a very famous story about a boy who did not want to grow up. *Peter Pan* wanted to stay as a boy, having fun in Never-Never land all the time. We cannot be like Peter Pan. Growing up is not always comfortable or easy, but we cannot stay as children all our lives. We move on to other interests and meet different people. As we grow older we take on more responsibilities but we also have the chance to learn many exciting things. Whatever the changes, we do not need to be alone. God has promised that he will be with us.

After Jesus left them, the disciples had to learn to cope without him there in person. The disciples were moving on, but Jesus did not leave them without help. They had the Holy Spirit with them which made them strong and confident. The Apostles moved away from their base in Jerusalem. They left their friends behind and went out to tell others all about their greatest friend, Jesus. That is what the name Apostle meant. Philip set off for Samaria where he met a stranger.

STORY

> Philip and the Ethiopian
> Acts 8:4-6, 26-40
> The man from Africa (p. 197)

Think of all the new skills, subjects and pastimes that you may learn and enjoy, or would like to learn and enjoy, in the next year. What other new things will meet you around the corner? — new friends, different school, new house, etc.? Whatever happens, God will be there with you.

ACTIVITIES

Memories scrap book
You may remember all or some of the festivals and seasons looked at through this last year. Items could include:

- Harvest

- Remembrance Sunday

- Christingle
- Christmas
- Candlemas
- Shrove Tuesday
- Lent
- Palm Sunday
- Good Friday
- All Saints
- Advent
- Hanukah
- New Year and Epiphany
- Ash Wednesday
- Mothering Sunday
- Maundy Thursday
- Easter
- Passover
- Christian Aid Week
- Shavuot
- Trinity
- Ascension
- Pentecost
- Birthdays
- Baptism
- Wedding
- Saints — Andrew, David, Patrick, George, Peter
- Flower Festival
- Holidays

Use symbols or pictures to recall each of these festivals and memories. Make a scrap book, drawing pictures or symbols, or writing a short description.

Pop-up festival book

The same thing can be done with a pop-up book. Make them like the cards for Mothering Sunday (session 22). Draw the picture/symbol on card and cut it out. Fold an A4 sheet of card in half. Cut twice through the folded side for about 6 cm. and push this inside out to make a step. Stick the picture onto the step. Stick the cards together to make a book.

Festival zig-zag

You will need:
- *a long, narrow sheet of stiff paper or thin card*
- *crayons/felt pens*
- *scissors*
- *glue*

Fold the long sheet of paper (smaller pieces may be stuck together) into a zig-zag with twelve sections. At the top of each section, write one of the following, in order:

> Advent, Christmas, Epiphany, Ash Wednesday, Lent, Mothering Sunday, Palm Sunday, Maundy Thursday, Good Friday, Easter, Ascension, Pentecost

The list may be added to or deleted to fit your requirements. Illustrate each section with a picture or symbol to show what is remembered on that day or in that season.

PRAYER AND PRAISE

When we celebrate, we may have a party. Sometimes at parties we have balloons. Blow up lots of coloured balloons. On each balloon draw with felt pen or ballpoint pen symbols or pictures of some of the things that you remember from the past year, or concerns for the next year.

In a time of quiet, the balloons may be tossed into the centre while you think and pray about what you have put on the balloon. You may like to say that out loud, but God knows what you want to say if you prefer to remain

silent. Collect the balloons and tie them up high for others to see them later.

Send us out into the world in the power of your Spirit to live and work to your praise and glory. Go in peace to love and serve the Lord.

92 I do not know what lies ahead
172 Now be strong
188 One more step along the world
249 There's new life in Jesus
279 When the road is rough
369 I cast all my cares upon you
381 I'm going to take a step
429 Maybe you can't draw or sing
468 The journey of life

PUZZLE ANSWERS

Answers to Crossword

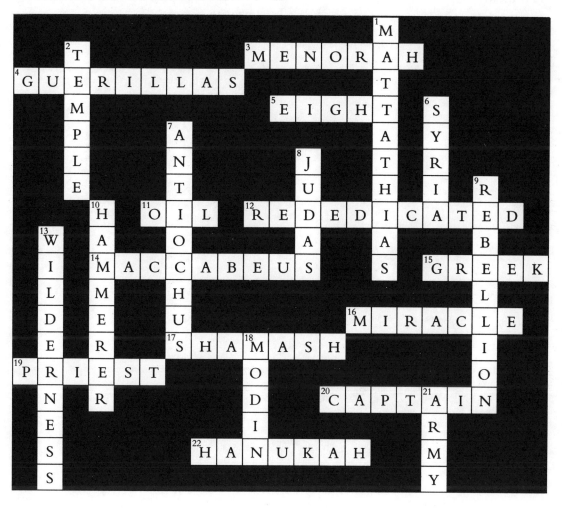

Across

3. Menorah
4. Guerillas
5. Eight
11. Oil
12. Rededicated
14. Maccabeus
15. Greek
16. Miracle
17. Shamash
19. Priest
20. Captain
22. Hanukah

Down

1. Mattathias
2. Temple
6. Syria
7. Antiochus
8. Judas
9. Rebellion
10. Hammerer
13. Wilderness
18. Modin
21. Army

Answers to Blockbusters

A	Andrew	M	Matthew
B	Bethany	N	Nicodemus
C	Capernaum	O	Olives
D	Donkey	P	Peter
E	Egypt	R	Rome
F	Five Thousand	S	Sadducees
G	Galilee	T	Temple
H	Herod	V	Vine
I	Inn	W	Wilderness
J	Jairus	Y	Yoke
K	Kidron	Z	Zacchaeus
L	Lazarus		